Student Loans:
A Parent's Guide

Table of Contents

Introduction

In March, 2012, the Federal Reserve Bank of New York caught the public's attention when it announced that student loan debt had surpassed credit card debt in the U.S. for the first time. While other types of debt have steadily decreased since consumer debt peaked in 2008, student loan debt continues to grow. Approximately 60 percent of college students now borrow annually to pay for their educations. Economists question what this will mean for the U.S. economy and how the burden of student loan debt will affect the lives of our children. Studies already show that student loan debt is a factor in choosing a career, buying a home, and deciding whether and when to get married.

Almost every week, news media features an article about the impact of student loan debt on young graduates. These articles rarely discuss the financial effect of student loan debt on the students' parents. A young person making a monthly student loan payment of several hundred dollars is unable to set aside money for emergencies, like car repairs or medical expenses. When such a crisis occurs, parents often step in to help pay the bills. Student loan debt also makes it harder for young graduates to move out of their parents' homes and set up their own households. The additional financial burden affects parents' retirement savings, and sometimes draws resources away the education of younger brothers and sisters.

A college education today costs as much as buying a house. It could be the largest purchase in a student's lifetime. Most adults would not make an important financial investment without carefully evaluating their finances and planning how they will manage the payments, yet we are allowing millions of 17- and 18-year-olds with little or no financial expertise to take on exactly that kind of commitment. As a parent, you cannot expect to control every aspect of your child's life, or to dictate what career path your child will follow. At the same time, you want to protect your children from heartache and disappointment, and from a life of financial hardship. There is a delicate balance between letting your children learn to make adult decisions and face the consequences, and imposing the benefit of your own knowledge and experience so that their mistakes do not mar their lives.

Once a student has been accepted by a college, university, or other learning institution, it is relatively easy to obtain student loans. Most students eagerly sign the necessary documents without giving a thought to the future. Though university financial aid departments provide educational materials, legal disclosures, financial advice, and exit counseling when a student leaves school, this information passes right over the heads of many students. While older adults are concerned about interest rates and repayment options, students are preoccupied with choosing their classes and finding a place to live, and are just grateful to be able to fund their educations.

Many parents are equally unaware of the consequences of borrowing to pay for education, until their children find themselves in some kind of difficulty at school or are faced with repayment six months after graduation.

Student loans can be sound financial investments when they are used in the right way. Government student loans offer reasonable interest rates and a variety of repayment options that do not exist for other types of loans. Student loans allow talented 17-year-olds with no credit history to invest in their futures and get the qualifications they need for professional careers. They also allow students from low-income families to attend college alongside more privileged young people and to compete based on intellect and ability. An economist or financial planner can demonstrate that a student loan is a good financial tool when it is well-managed. To get the most value from student loans, however, you must know their limitations and the risks involved.

Student loans are financial products, marketed to the public just like credit cards and mortgages. Investors buy and sell student debt and make money from the interest. Schools depend on student loan money to boost their enrollment and partially fund many of their students' education expenses. The information that is fed to the public about student loans is designed to appeal to students and parents and convince them to take on debt. It is important to look beyond the publicity and understand student loans for what they really are. A student loan can convey great benefits when it is managed well, but it can also lead a family into financial pitfalls from which it is difficult to recover.

Federal and state student loans, funded and managed by the government, are subject to strict requirements and regulations. The information reported on your income tax returns determines the types and amounts of government loans for which your student is eligible. Government student loans offer a number of repayment options and some cancellation benefits that reward students for pursuing certain public service careers. The private student loans available through banks and financial institutions have some of the same features as federal loans, but do not offer the same benefits. Parents and students should be aware of the types of student loans they are receiving. Government student loans have an annual loan limit which often does not cover the full cost of a year at school, so that parents and students have to seek additional funding through scholarships, grants, Parent PLUS loans, and private student loans.

As a parent of three recent college graduates, I know how college expenses affect family finances, and the impact of student loans on the choices children make about their educations and their careers. This book will help you navigate the challenges of funding your child's education. It explains the financial implications of student loan debt, the different types of government and private student loans, and what happens when you cosign a loan for your child. Evaluate the commitment you are making when you borrow money to pay for education. Investigate how you can get additional funding for education, such as scholarships and grants, and how you can save money on college expenses. Learn how to make the most of your student's college experience. Educate yourself and your child about borrowing student loans, and discover how you can help your child plan for life after college. Find out how education expenses and student loan interest can reduce your taxes.

Each chapter provides an overview of one aspect of student loans. When you find information which applies to your particular situation, do more research and seek assistance from a financial aid officer, accountant, or counselor if you need it. At the end of this book is a list of organizations and web sites where you can find information about financial aid and student loans. Universities and the federal and state

3

governments provide a range of free resources to help you get student loans, manage your financial obligations, and succeed in school. Never leave your questions unanswered. Keep asking until you understand.

No two families are alike. This book will help you identify the concerns of your particular student and craft a unique financial solution for your family that will provide your child with a college education .

Chapter 1: What Student Loans Mean for Your Family

Student loans mean that your intelligent and talented son or daughter can go to college even when your family cannot afford to pay for it. A four-year college education today can easily cost between $60,000 and $170,000, depending on which school your child attends, how many years he or she stays there, and whether or not your child lives at home while in school. In the 17 or 18 years between the birth of a child and high school graduation, many families would have difficulty saving this amount, in addition to paying rent or a mortgage, paying for insurance, buying and maintaining one or more cars, and saving for retirement. Many parents of today's students have experienced several years of underemployment or unemployment, and may have lost homes to foreclosure. Divorced or single parents have to bear the expense of maintaining a household with only one income. Families with two or more high-school-aged children have a double or triple financial burden. Without student loans to cover at least part of the expense, many families could not send their children to college.

When a student accepts a loan, he or she signs a promissory note agreeing to repay the loan over a 10- to 25- year period starting six months after leaving school. The concept is that after graduation, the student will be able to find a good job within six months and start paying off the loans. If your child does not start making payments on time, or misses payments, and does not make arrangements to delay payment (see *Forbearance* in *Chapter 1*), the loan will go into default, causing his or her credit rating to plunge. This could affect your child's efforts to find employment, and will prevent him or her from receiving additional education loans until payment arrangements have been made. As a responsible parent, you should know about your child's financial obligations. Make sure your child understands repayment terms and the amount of the repayment, and knows what to do if he or she is unable to make the monthly payments.

Unless you cosigned a student loan, your child is the person legally responsible for the student loan debt. However, if your child has difficulty finding suitable employment, you might find yourself making loan payments on his or her behalf. You might want to pay off some of the student loan debt yourself, or prevent your son or daughter's credit score from dropping. There could be times when your child is between jobs or is experiencing financial difficulties, and might need help with one or two loan payments. Though a student borrower can request temporary forbearance, there is a limit to the period of forbearance and sometimes a one-time fee. You could find yourself spending dollars that would otherwise go into your retirement savings, or towards other family needs, on your child's student loan payments.

Most student loans are disbursed directly to the student. Typically, the college or university receives the loan money from the lender, takes out the amount of tuition, room and board, and any other fees billed by the school, and deposits whatever is left in your child's bank account. Your child then decides how to spend that money. College is the first experience of independent living for many students. A 17- or 18-year-old may not know how to plan and stick to a budget, or how to set financial priorities. Your child probably will not consult you before spending money for extravagances that he or she will end up paying interest on for years to come. If your child is renting an apartment or house off campus, you might end up helping to pay the bills when the loan money runs out towards the end of the semester.

Government student loans are written off if the borrower dies before the loan is paid off. Responsibility for some private student loans, however, passes on to the borrower's heirs. If your child has taken out private student loans, there is a risk that you or your child's spouse and children could become financially obligated to pay them off.

What Student Loans Mean for Your Child

Student loans mean that your child can attend college, obtain a degree, and launch a fulfilling professional career. Studies by the Georgetown University Center on Education and the Workforce found that, on average, a Bachelor's degree holder earns 84 percent more over his or her lifetime than someone who only graduated from high school. Studies also show that people with college degrees are more satisfied with their jobs, healthier, and more likely to read to their children and prepare them for successful academic careers.

When your child graduates, however, he or she enters the real world with a substantial debt scheduled to be paid off over the next 10 years. Depending on how much was borrowed and the repayment schedule, the monthly payment can range from $100 to over $1,000. This is equivalent to a monthly car payment, or even a mortgage payment. Your child will have to delay major financial commitments, like buying a car or buying a home, until he or she is earning enough monthly income to pay for both.

Student loan debt also affects important personal decisions, such as whether and when to marry or have children. Though a marriage partner is not responsible for a spouse's student loans, the couple's combined income will be diminished by student loan payments. If the couple is considering a move that will further one spouse's career but reduce the other spouse's income, or if one spouse is leaving the workforce to care for children, arrangements have to be made for the student loan payments. A recent graduate with heavy loan debt may be reluctant to commit to marriage, feeling that it is important to establish a career and a secure income first.

After graduation, a borrower is given a six-month grace period to look for employment before the first payment is due. This limits the freedom to do some of the things recent college graduates traditionally do, such as travel or volunteer to gain work experience. Many exciting internships with non-profit organizations are unpaid. A college graduate with debt to pay off is under pressure to find a real job quickly, and might not have time to research and apply for the jobs best suited to his or her chosen profession. There is also a psychological element. A young person trying to break into the professional working world is likely to feel even more discouraged and disheartened when he or she does not find a job right away, worrying about the debt that must be paid off.

If you take a look at the statement for your child's student loan, you will find that after it is paid off for 10 years with interest, that $16,000 education actually cost $45,000. Inflation will lower the value of the dollar as the years pass, and you can avoid some of the interest by paying off the loan early. The reality, though, is that when you pay for education with a student loan, you are paying almost double the actual price of going to school.

The Difference Between a Student Loan and a Personal Loan

A student loan is a personal loan made to a student to pay for education expenses. The collateral for a student loan is the student. It is assumed that education will increase the student's earning potential, and that a student who earns good grades and qualifies to enter a university is a responsible person who will pay the loan back. Most student loans are not approved until the student's enrollment has been verified by the school.

Student loans guaranteed by the federal government are not based on the student's financial track record; most students are too young to have a meaningful credit score. The interest rate on federal student loans is calculated according to the current market rates. Interest rates for private student loans are based on the student's or cosigner's credit score, and can be very high.

The student is not required to start repaying a student loan as long as he or she is in school more than half time, and is given a six-month grace period after leaving school before the first payment is due. Student loans offer repayment options not available with other types of personal loans, such as deferment if the student returns to school, and limited forbearance during periods of economic hardship.

Financial planners often classify "good debt" and "bad debt". Good debt is money borrowed to purchase an asset that will increase in value over time, or generate income in some way. Bad debt is money borrowed to pay for something that will either be consumed or lose value over time. A student loan is good debt when it accomplishes its purpose – preparing the student for a career and a fulfilling life. Student loans become bad debt when they are not managed well – for example, when a student drops out before completing a course of study, or when the cost of school is out of proportion to the amount the graduate will earn afterwards. As consumers, you and your student are responsible for understanding the financial implications of student loan debt and making informed choices.

Should Your Child Go to College?

One of the debates surrounding student loans and higher education is whether so many young people really need to go to college in order to succeed in life. While it is possible to develop a lucrative career without acquiring a degree, statistical studies show that people who attend college are more productive and better-paid members of the labor force, healthier, and more satisfied with their lives than people who do not. This is not because they are more intelligent or talented than other people to begin with, but because the experience of going to college changes and enriches a person. A college education exposes students to knowledge and information, and expands their understanding of the world. In addition to book knowledge, college teaches valuable skills such as how to do research, write and communicate, and interact with many types of people.

A college degree is a plus in most professions. Many jobs require a bachelor's degree. Even if your child is accepted for an entry-level job without any higher education, a college degree is probably required for promotion or advancement to a management position.

Higher education includes trade schools and technical training. Someone who wants to become a sound technician, computer programmer, pastry chef, hotel manager, construction contractor, or photographer can get the necessary training at a trade school or community college. Your child might not have to go away to an expensive college or university to get a professional degree or certification. Research the educational options available in your community. Your student could shave thousands of dollars off the cost of an education by living at home while attending school.

Anyone of any age can get a student loan and earn a degree, but the year after high school is a good time to begin a course of higher education. Your child is accustomed to studying, attending classes, and completing assignments. Most recent high school graduates do not yet have families or other responsibilities that might distract them from their studies. As a first-year college freshman, your child will be surrounded by students who are mostly of a similar age and level of maturity, providing opportunities to form friendships and to develop and grow along with his or her peers.

The value of a college education is undeniable. The important thing is to make sure the education you receive is appropriate and worth the price, particularly when you are borrowing to pay for it. Consider whether your child's projected career field will earn enough to pay off the loans without financial hardship. If your child plans to become a social worker, for example, do not take out student loans to go to an expensive private college. Research your college options carefully to choose a school that matches your child's interests and abilities. A student does not have to be an academic superstar to succeed in college or professional school, if placed in the right environment. If your child is motivated to get a higher education, look for a school that will offer enough challenge without overwhelming him or her.

For-Profit Colleges and Student Loans

For-profit colleges market themselves aggressively to low-income students and nontraditional students such as non-English speakers and older workers who want to change careers. They advertise on television, and entice students with promises of higher-paying jobs that will provide better lives for their families. In fact, their tuition rates are often double or triple the tuition for similar courses at community colleges and private universities, and student loan debt more than cancels out any additional income a student might gain by graduating from a course. Many students drop out or fail to get good jobs when they graduate, and end up floundering student loan debt.

For-profit schools rely heavily on student loans for their income, and consequently their admissions officers often use high-pressure tactics to get students to sign loan documents. These include suggesting that there is a now-or-never deadline and the student must decide right away, and persuasive bullying with comments like, "Come on! You don't want to be a loser. Turn your life around right now!" The federal government is currently investigating predatory lending practices such as not revealing the actual cost of tuition until after the loan documents are signed, falsifying documents to qualify for loans, and steering students to high-interest loans from "preferred lenders".

Only 9 percent of all college students in the U.S. attend for-profit institutions, but they receive approximately 25 percent of all federal Pell grants and loans, and are responsible for 44 percent of student loan defaults. New federal regulations announced in March, 2014, require for-profit schools to demonstrate that their graduates' debt load does not exceed 8 percent of their total income in order to receive federal financial aid money.

For-profit schools include familiar names like University of Phoenix, DeVry University, Everest College, and Kaplan College, but they also include many types of technical training schools. If your student is considering attending a for-profit school, investigate the cost of similar courses at a local state or community college. Do not allow your student to be pressured into making a decision. If you suspect a school is using deceptive advertising to recruit students to your state Department of Consumer Affairs.

Chapter 2: Your Action Plan

It is never too early to start planning for college – many families begin setting aside a college fund or paying into a prepaid tuition plan as soon as a child is born. If you intend to use financial aid or student loans to help pay for your college-bound high school student's education, do not wait until the last semester of senior year to begin researching your options.

The process of getting your child through college will occupy your mind and affect your finances for at least six years of your life. Though you cannot make all of your child's decisions and control every aspect of his or her behavior, you can try to anticipate the direction your child will take and your financial needs for college. As a parent, you can support your high school student's college ambitions by learning about scholarship opportunities and educational requirements, making sure deadlines are met and applications are filed on time, and providing transportation and financial help so that your student can participate in classes, exams, sports, and volunteer activities. All of these will help make your student look well-rounded on college applications and increase his or her chances of being accepted by a university.

During last two years of high school, you can prepare financially by setting aside savings for college expenses, paying off credit card debt, and planning carefully for any large financial transactions such as the purchase or sale of a house or car. Large balances in your checking or savings accounts when you submit your Free Application for Federal Student Aid (FAFSA) will reduce your student's eligibility for financial aid and certain types of loans.

A student loan is a financial investment that will bring the best return if your student completes his or her college courses and graduates with a degree. Your student is more likely to succeed in college if he or she is emotionally and physically prepared. During the last years of high school, teach your child how to make a budget and manage money. Encourage your child to become independent through work and community service experiences, internships, and periods of traveling or living away from home. Work with your child to create a plan for managing health issues while at college. Be aware of personal habits that could cause problems for your child in college, such as difficulty managing time or excessive involvement in online gaming or social networking. If you suspect your child has a tendency to abuse drugs or alcohol, seek counseling before he or she goes away to school.

High School - Junior Year

Your child's junior year in high school is an important time to begin preparations for college and take steps to maximize your eligibility for scholarships, financial aid, and federal and state student loans.

Keep up academic performance.
A student's high school grade point average or SAT score does not affect eligibility for federal financial aid or student loans. It does affect eligibility for merit-based financial aid, including scholarships offered through schools, state programs such as the Florida Bright Futures scholarship, and private scholarships. A higher grade point average increases the likelihood that your student will get free money for education and need to borrow less. A high grade point average also increases your child's chances of being accepted at the school of his or her choice.

Help your child stay on track at school. If your child has been making poor grades, there is still time to turn the situation around. If your child has talent but lacks motivation, seriously consider what can be done to get him or her more involved in schoolwork. Does your child need extra tutoring or more attention from teachers? Are social situations and friends a distraction? As a parent you might not be able to interfere in your child's social life or force your child to study, but you can look for the underlying reasons why your child is participating in certain types of behavior. It could be that your child needs more intellectual challenges, or needs experiences to build self-confidence and awareness of the wider world outside high school. Many school districts now offer some or all of their classes online, allowing students more flexibility and the opportunity to work at their own pace. A job or internship can help your student develop practical skills and new social contacts. If your child has a special interest, such as computer

14

technology or art, consider enrolling him or her in workshops or community college classes. Many high schools incorporate community college classes in their curriculums. Poor performance in high school does not prevent a student from succeeding academically later in life, but it shuts him or her out of many educational opportunities that are easily available to recent high school graduates.

Register for Advanced Placement (AP) courses.

High school students can take college-level Advance Placement (AP) courses. These courses, available for 30 subjects, stand out on a college application and show that a student has taken rigorous classes and demonstrated the skills necessary to succeed in college. If the student achieves a high score on the final exam, many universities accept the AP course as a college credit. By taking AP courses in high school, a student can fulfill some of the university's general education requirements and either graduate early or add an additional major or minor to his or her college degree. AP courses also give high school students a taste of various fields of study such as literature, psychology, law, or science, and allow them to explore possible majors.

Prepare for and take the SAT and ACT.

Most students take the ACT or SAT assessments for the first time during the spring of their junior year in high school, and many take it a second time in the fall of their senior year. The student can submit the higher of the two scores on college applications. At many universities, including those that offer full scholarships to low-income students, SAT and ACT scores are an important factor in deciding whether a student will be accepted. The ACT and SAT, which are intended to assess a student's readiness for college, are heavily weighted towards reading and writing skills and knowledge of vocabulary. Your child can often improve an SAT or ACT score by learning test-taking skills, memorizing vocabulary words, and practicing with SAT and ACT software. High schools often offer classes, free software, and discounts on SAT training software to help their students raise their SAT scores.

Volunteer for community service.

Many scholarships require the student to perform a specified number of hours of community service work. Involvement in community service projects also looks good on a college application, and gives your child an opportunity to develop self-confidence, and acquire work experience and leadership skills. Since college applications are generally submitted at the beginning of the senior year, the junior year is the best time to volunteer for community service opportunities.

Apply for scholarships.
Your student should consult a high school guidance counselor about possible scholarships and the timelines for applying. Some applications must be submitted during the summer of the junior year, and some scholarships require participation in activities that involve time and planning. Search for scholarships online, and find out whether your employer offers scholarships for families of employees.

Visit colleges.
Junior year is also a good time to visit colleges. Touring college campuses gives you and your child a feel for the academic environment and the student population at each school, and improves your chances of finding a school that is a good fit. As explained in *Chapter 6: Making the Most of Your College Dollars*, a student who is dissatisfied with a school is more likely to fail classes or drop out, increasing the risks associated with borrowing student loans.

Plan for income tax strategies.
The tax year that begins in January of your child's junior year in high school is your "base year" for determining financial aid eligibility. The tax information for that year is what you will enter on your first FAFSA, in the first months of the year that your child will start college. See *Chapter 4: Filling Out Your FAFSA* for strategies that might help you qualify for a larger amount of financial aid.

High School - Senior Year

Pay attention to deadlines.
The fall of your child's senior year is when your student will take the SAT or ACT again, fill out college applications, and apply for scholarships. Pay attention to application deadlines. Your student should work closely with a high school guidance counselor to learn about scholarships offered by local organizations, and to fulfill all the requirements for state financial aid programs.

Evaluate your finances.

Take some time to revisit your finances and to determine how much money you will need for your child's first year in college.

Mr. and Mrs. D are divorced. Their son qualified for the Florida Bright Futures program, which pays a percentage of college tuition for Florida residents, and various minor scholarships. After applying for the maximum in federal student loans, they agreed to each pay half of the remaining Cost of Attendance (COA) so that their son, a talented trumpet player and band choreographer, could attend Stetson University, a private university in Florida recognized for its music programs, where the annual tuition is over $32,000. Their son loved school and was immediately invited to join the orchestra after his first audition. After the start of the second semester, though, Mrs. D was unable to afford her share of the cost. The orchestra director could not find funding for a scholarship so late in the academic year. Three weeks into the second semester, the son had to withdraw from classes, pack up his belongings, say goodbye to his new friends, and go home to wait until the next academic year, when he could enter a less expensive state university. (His ability was quickly recognized at the state university, where he became a paid assistant to the band director.)

Get your personal records in order.

Make sure the name on your child's Social Security card matches the name your child's birth certificate. If there are any discrepancies or problems, make an appointment with your local Social Security office and resolve them now. Incorrect Social Security information could delay processing of your FAFSA or disbursement of financial aid and work study wages when your child starts college.

If you do not already have them on file, get copies of your child's up-to-date vaccination records, and of any documents pertaining to citizenship status or residence in your state.

Our daughter's first and middle names were reversed on her Social Security card. No one noticed until she got to college and started filling out forms for a paid internship. In the middle of her busy class schedule, she had to make a long bus trip to the Social Security office and wait for hours in line. On her first visit, she was informed that she needed to come back with a certified copy of her birth certificate, which we had to send by overnight mail. The whole incident embarrassed her, cost her hours of precious time, and delayed her first paycheck by two weeks.

Fill out the FAFSA.
The Free Application for Federal Student Aid (FAFSA) is typically available to fill out online starting in mid-January. You and your student should fill out your FAFSA as early as you can. Do not wait until you have finished doing your taxes; use the worksheet to estimate your taxes and go back enter the correct amounts when you have completed your tax return. Enter the names of all the schools your student is applying to. Schools have limited amounts of federal and state funds for certain types of need-based financial aid such as the Federal Supplemental Educational Opportunity Grant (FSEOG) and work study programs. Submitting your FAFSA early increases your chances of being awarded these types of financial aid, which are allotted on a first-come, first-serve basis. See *Chapter 4: Filling Out Your FAFSA*.

Compare financial aid award letters.
When your student receives financial aid award letters from the colleges to which he or she has been accepted, compare them carefully before making a final decision. See the section on award letters in *Chapter 3: Understanding Financial Aid and Student Loan Options*.

Follow the school's instructions and deadlines.
When your student decides which school he or she will attend, follow all the school's instructions for accepting financial aid and student loans. Sign the Master Promissory Note (MPN), take the entrance counseling, and supply bank account information for direct deposit or a mailing address where disbursement checks can be sent, and contact information for the loan servicer. It is best to provide the parents' home address to the loan servicer since the student will be living in dorms and moving from one address to another.

Calculate your student's financial requirements for freshman year.
Look over your student's financial aid award letter and make sure you understand each of the items. Visit or call the financial aid office and get answers to all your questions. If the financial aid awards do not cover all the cost, and you cannot afford to pay, talk to a financial aid officer. Your family circumstances might qualify your student for bigger loans or financial aid awards, or you might need to apply for a Parent PLUS loan to make up the difference. You can only borrow enough in federal and state loans to make up the amount of the school's COA. Your student's actual expenses living off-campus or taking extra classes might be more than the school estimates in its COA. You might need extra money if your student has to fly a long distance to attend the school, or if your student has to purchase additional equipment and supplies. Plan for your family's travel expenses to attend student orientation and help your student move in.

Keep up your student's GPA.
Make sure your student keeps up his or her grade point average (GPA) during that senior year. Though it does not affect federal financial aid or student loans, a low GPA during the senior year could disqualify the student from state and school merit-based financial aid.

Pay attention at freshman orientation.
Most schools host a mandatory freshman orientation for parents and students. It is important for one or both parents to attend this orientation, because the school takes this opportunity to inform the parents about its policies and procedures. For parents, a typical orientation includes an introduction to the school and some of its staff, a campus tour, sampling of the campus food plans, information about

campus security and dormitory rules, seminars about how to support students, and question and answer sessions. For incoming students, the orientation often includes issuing student ID cards, registering for classes, and other important procedures. Pay attention. Though some of the information may not seem relevant now, it could help you later when your student is in a difficulty of one kind or another. This is a good opportunity to meet with a financial aid officer, learn more about the majors and programs offered at the school, and collect printed information such as contact phone numbers and school policies.

Register for classes.
Follow the school's procedure for registering for classes. For incoming freshmen, this is typically done at the freshman orientation.
Enrollment for many classes is limited. The sooner a student registers, the more likely that he or she will get into the classes required for a particular major. Uncertainty about class registration can contribute to a student's emotional turmoil and confusion at the beginning of the first semester, and make it more difficult for a new student to successfully adjust to school.

Open a bank account for your student.
If your student does not already have a bank account, open one now. Having a bank account to receive student loan disbursements will speed up the process and make it easier for your student to keep track of expenditures. If your student gives you the account passwords, you will be able to monitor his or her spending. (You cannot control your student's bank account, but you can give helpful advice.) Make sure the bank has branches and ATM machines in the city where your child will be going to school. Many universities partner with a specific bank that has a branch on campus, and turn student ID cards into debit cards. Though you are not required to use the school's preferred bank, it is convenient to be able to stop in at the bank between classes, and these banks have staff who are friendly and sympathetic to a student's needs.

Freshman Year of College

Plan for extra cash.
In the fall of your student's freshman year, you will need extra money to buy school supplies, and bedding and furnishings for the dormitory.

Your freshman might not receive a student loan disbursement to help with personal expenses until 30 days after the beginning of the first semester. Your family will have hotel and travel expenses when you go to help your student move in, or when you visit for a parent's weekend or a football game. Your student might need to purchase a new computer or cell phone plan.

Mr. and Mrs. J were very proud when their son received a football scholarship at a smaller state university. Determined to give him their full support, they vowed to attend every game. After driving hundreds of miles to the first two away games, and paying for motel rooms and meals for their family and the son's girlfriend, they realized that their enthusiasm was driving them into debt. Since their son was a freshman, he spent very little time on the field. Much as they wanted to be there to see him in action, they decided to limit their attendance to home games and championships.

Start a student loan binder.
Soon after your student's loans are disbursed, you will begin receiving letters or electronic notices from your student's loan servicer. These contain information about interest rates, disbursement dates, and accrued interest. Store these in a binder or a folder on your computer. These notifications are legal documents from the loan servicer and you might need to refer to them later.

Monitor and coach your student.
Without interfering too much, question your student during the first weeks of the semester to find out if he or she is attending classes, if student loan money has been disbursed, and if your student has any concerns or difficulties. Encourage your student to talk to a financial aid officer or an academic advisor and get problems resolved. If necessary, you can make a phone call and get some information yourself, but your student is the one who has to make decisions, fill out applications, and sign forms.

A school has many resources to assist students who ask for help. During those years at college, your student will encounter a variety of challenges such as changing majors, failing grades, and difficulty in registering for required classes. With a little encouragement at the beginning, your student will become adept at navigating the school's policies, procedures, and deadlines. Failure to act could cost you money. A low GPA or too many failed classes will disqualify a student for financial aid and increase the amount you have to borrow in student loans or pay out of pocket. If you student takes more than 150 percent of the time required to complete a major, financial aid and federal loan eligibility will expire.

Fill out your FAFSA early.

You and your student must fill out your FAFSA every year. From now on it will be easier, because much of the information remains the same, and you can use the IRS Data Retrieval Tool (IRS DRT) to transfer details from your tax return. Be sure to update the number of family members attending college and any other circumstances that might have changed for that year.

Second and Following Years in College

Keep up with your student loan information.

Continue to read and file away the notices that arrive from your student loan servicer. During senior year, be aware of approaching student loan limits. If your student has been borrowing the full amount of Subsidized Direct and Unsubsidized Direct loans for four years, only $4,000 will be available for a fifth year. Typically, the amount awarded in grants and scholarships is reduced during the later years in school, making it necessary to borrow larger amounts than previously.

Stay on track for your major.

The school determines how many credit hours or semesters are required to complete each of its majors. Your student is eligible to receive federal financial aid and student loans for 150 percent of the time it takes to complete a major. When the student switches from one major to another that requires more semesters or credit hours, the time already completed in the first major is counted as part of the new limit. Your student may need to plan ahead and register early to get access to all the classes required for the major. As your student approach the end of his or her studies, keep track of credit hours to avoid unpleasant surprises.

Fill out your FAFSA.
Continue to fill out your FAFSA early each year. Remember that financial aid distributed by the school, such as work-study, might be awarded on a first-come, first-serve basis.

Apply for a Parent PLUS loan.
If the federal and state loans do not cover all the cost of your child's education that year, you can apply for a Parent PLUS loan to make up the difference. If you apply and do not qualify for a Parent PLUS loan, your student may be eligible for additional financial aid and student loan amounts. If your application qualifies, follow the steps to complete acceptance of the loan.

Year That Student Graduates or Leaves School

Complete exit counseling.
Your student will be required to complete an exit counseling session, either online or in person with a school financial aid officer.

Gather all your student's loan information.
Gather all your student's loan information in one place. Create a list or spreadsheet of all your loans, including any private loans or dedicated credit lines that you used to pay only for education expenses.

Plan for your student's grace period.
Borrowers of student loans are given a six-month grace period before they must begin paying back student loans. The grace period begins the day that the student officially "separates" from school. The loan servicer will notify you of the first payment amount and the date when it is due. Mark this date on your calendar. If your student has not found regular employment by the end of the grace period, you might need to help him or her negotiate repayment options. If you anticipate that the student will be able to make regular loan payments after one or two more months, you might prefer to help out with loan payments than have your student enter forbearance. See *Chapter 7: Repaying Your Student Loans.*

Pay the accrued interest.
Before the end of the grace period, the student has the option of paying the accrued interest before the loan goes into repayment. Otherwise,

the interest is added to loan capital and interest is paid on it over the life of the loan. If your student can pay the accrued interest at this time, he or she can save money and slightly reduce the amount of the monthly loan payment.

Make plans for repaying the student loan.
Your student's choice of job opportunities, internships, and living arrangements will all be affected by student loan debt. He or she could go to graduate school and re-enter student loan deferment, or enter military service and get some of the loan paid off. If the student wants to take time off to travel or do an unpaid internship, he or she will have to come up with a means of making loan payments when the grace period ends. The pressure is on to find a job with a salary sufficient to pay off the loans.

Year After Graduating or Leaving School

Begin paying off the student loan.
If the six-month grace period has not already ended, it will end this year and the student must make arrangements to begin loan payments.

Claim education tax benefits for the last time.
A student who is no longer in school full time cannot be claimed as a dependent on the parents' tax return unless they provide more than half of his or her support. Whether the student is a dependent on this year's tax return will depend on the graduation date and how much support the parents provided. If a student is not the parents' dependent, they cannot take the American opportunity credit, lifetime learning credit, or tuition and fees deduction for education expenses.

Begin taking the student loan interest tax deduction.
A person who is not a dependent on someone else's tax return can take the student loan interest tax deduction. A child who is out of school is no longer a dependent unless you provide more than half of the financial support. If your child does not qualify as your dependent, he or she can take the student loan interest deduction. It does not matter who actually made the loan payments; the person legally responsible for paying back the loan claims the deduction. If a relative such as a grandparent wants to help with education expenses by paying off student loans, it is wise to wait until the student is no longer a

dependent so that he or she can take the student loan interest deduction for those payments.

Following Years

Continue making student loan payments.
Defaulting on a student loan has serious consequences, and late payments may cause your student to lose the benefit of repayment incentives, incur late fees, and affect his or her credit score. Borrowers who have difficulty making student loan payments should keep in contact with their student loan servicers and use the various repayment options to manage their finances.

Keep track of any loan forgiveness programs.
A borrower who qualifies for federal Public Service Loan Forgiveness, or deferment and loan forgiveness through active military service or a federal program such as AmeriCorps or the Peace Corps, should keep track of these benefits and fill out the necessary applications and forms. Most of these benefits are not distributed automatically. The burden is on the student to apply for these program and provide the necessary documentation.

Inquire about education benefits available through employers. Some federal and state agencies offer student loan forgiveness as employment incentives. If you are enlisting for military service, discuss education benefits with your recruiter. Some states have loan forgiveness programs for teachers and health care workers in areas of need.

Take the student loan interest tax deduction.
Every year at tax time, get your *Form 1098-E* from your loan servicer and enter the deduction on your tax return.

Chapter 3: Understanding Financial Aid and Student Loan Options

Every year, as many as two million families fail to fill out the FAFSA because they are unaware that they qualify for federal assistance with education expenses, or that they can borrow federal and state student loans to go to college. Never assume that you cannot afford to send your child to college. Though eligibility for financial aid is based primarily on family income, other qualifying factors include family size and number of students in college. Higher-income families that do not qualify for financial aid can apply for merit-based scholarships and borrow unsubsidized Direct student loans and Parent PLUS loans. When you are planning for your child's education, it is important to understand all the options available to your family.

The two types of education funding are financial aid and student loans.

Financial aid includes scholarships, grants, and subsidized federal and state student loans. Scholarships and grants are the most desirable type of financial aid because they do not have to be paid back and are essentially a gift. The federal government provides several need-based grants for low-income families, and many states do the same. Ask a high school guidance counselor or a college financial aid officer about need-based financial aid available in your state, or visit the website of your state higher education agency. Most state financial aid programs require you to be a state resident.

A variety of grants and scholarships are offered by states, individual schools, and private donors. These are based on financial need, academic merit, special circumstances, or a particular talent or interest. Most schools have scholarship funds that they distribute to students who meet certain requirements. Many scholarships from private donors have a complicated application process and some require the recipient to demonstrate financial need.

Subsidized student loans have to be paid back with interest after the student graduates, but while the student is in school the government pays the interest. This reduces the total amount the student must pay back over a 10- to 20-year period and can translate into thousands of dollars in savings over the years. Only lower-income families are eligible for subsidized student loans. There is a limit to the amount of subsidized loans a student can borrow each year, and many student need to borrow additional unsubsidized loans.

Unsubsidized federal and state student loans are available to all students, regardless of income. Federal and state student loans are guaranteed by the federal or a state government, making it possible for them to offer a low interest rate. Federal and state loans also offer in-school deferment, flexible repayment options and a variety of loan forgiveness programs tied to public service careers such as social work, teaching, and medicine. There is an annual limit on the amount of federal and state loans a student can borrow. If the student needs additional money, parents can borrow federal Parent PLUS student loans up to the school's estimated cost of attendance (COA).

Private student loans are offered by banks and financial institutions to students or their parents to pay for education. Private student loans offer several advantages over other types of private loans, including automatic eligibility once the student is accepted by a school and some special repayment options. Interest rates for private loans are based on market rates and the borrower or cosigner's credit score. Private student loans are not eligible for federal or state loan forgiveness programs.

NOTE: The process of getting a student loan is so streamlined that many students do not understand the seriousness of their debt obligation. Student loans, unlike other types of personal debt, are very difficult to discharge in bankruptcy. If you fail to make payments on federal Direct student loans, the government will garnish wages, tax refunds, and Social Security checks until repayment is reinstated.

The first step in applying for financial aid and government student loans is to fill out the Free Application for Federal Student Aid (FAFSA). Schools use the information on your FAFSA to calculate your Expected Family Contribution (EFC) and determine whether you qualify for need-based financial aid programs. The formula for determining eligibility for financial aid is complicated, and the only way to find out how much you qualify for is to apply. Your school will then put together a financial aid package that includes need-based financial aid if you are eligible, scholarships, grants, federal and state student loans, and federal work study amounts. This package is presented in an award letter to your student, who can accept or decline any part of the package.

Take advantage of all available grants and scholarships, and pay whatever you can afford out of your own pocket to keep your student's debt load as small as possible. Next, take out federal and state student loans. If you still need money, make up the shortfall with a federal Parent Loan for Undergraduate Students (PLUS). Private student loans should be a last resort because of their less favorable interest rates and repayment options.

How to Qualify for Financial Aid

Most U.S. students are eligible to receive some form of federal financial aid to help pay for college or career training, regardless of age, race, or field of study. To qualify for financial aid, a student must:

- Be a U.S. citizen or U.S. national, or hold a green card
- Be enrolled or accepted for enrollment as a regular student at an approved school
- Have a valid Social Security number (unless the student is from the Republic of the Marshall Islands, Federated States of Micronesia, or the Republic of Palau)
- If a male, be registered with the Selective Service (males must register between the ages of 18 and 25)
- Not be in default on a previous federal student loan or owe a refund on a federal grant (A student who is in default may become eligible by making payment arrangements and resuming payments on the previous loan)

- Sign a statement that the loan funds will be used for educational
-

Financial Aid for Undocumented Students

Under current policies, undocumented students cannot legally receive any federally funded student financial aid, including loans, grants, scholarships, and work study money.

No federal or state law prevents the admission of undocumented immigrants to public or private U.S. institutions of higher education. Individual institutions have different policies on admitting undocumented students. Though it not a state law, many four-year colleges in Virginia require proof of U.S. citizenship as a condition for admission. In other states, undocumented students are treated as foreign or out-of-state students and are charged the higher out-of-state tuition. According to the National Conference of State Legislatures, 14 states do offer in-state tuition to illegal immigrants who attended high school in the state. Only Texas, California, and New Mexico offer state financial aid to undocumented students.

For more than a decade, Congress has been debating the passage of a federal Development, Relief, and Education for Alien Minors (DREAM) Act. The DREAM Act provision of the Border Security, Economic Opportunity, and Immigration Modernization Act , S 744, passed by the Senate in June 2013, would allow young people who entered the country illegally to become U.S. citizens in six years if they attend college or serve in the military. AN amendment introduced by Senator Mazie K. Hirono, Democrat, of Hawaii, would make these students eligible for financial aid during this six-year period.

Educational Qualifications

Since July 1, 2012, to receive federal loans or grants, a student must have either a high school diploma or a General Educational Development (GED) certificate. or have completed a high school education in a home school setting approved under state law. The student must be enrolled or accepted for enrollment as a regular student in an eligible degree or certificate program, and must have been admitted through the school's regular admissions process.

NOTE: The Ability to Benefit (AtB) test no longer applies. Until July 1, 2012, students who did not have a high school diploma could qualify for federal financial aid by taking a federally approved AtB test demonstrating that they had the language and comprehension skills to benefit from a college education. In 2008, Congress implemented an additional option allowing a student without a high school diploma who completed at least 6 credit hours or 225 clock hours of postsecondary education to qualify for federal student financial aid. Pilot programs conducted through the Department of Education's Experimental Sites Initiative showed that student without high school diplomas or GEDs who received financial aid after completing 6 credits (without federal aid) academically outperformed students with high school diplomas in college. However, AtB provisions were eliminated by Congress in December 2011 with the *Constitutional Appropriations Act of Fiscal Year 2012*. Students enrolling in college after July 1, 2012, have not been able to become eligible for financial aid by taking an AtB test, and must instead get a GED certification.

Maintaining Satisfactory Academic Progress (SAP)

Qualifying for financial aid the first semester of freshman year is only the first step. Your student could lose eligibility for financial aid, subsidized Direct loans, and unsubsidized Direct loans if he or she does not keep up a minimum GPA, or fails or drops too many classes.

A conscientious student who follows a relatively smooth degree path will have little difficulty remaining eligible for federal financial aid until graduation. If your student fails or drops too many classes, or changes majors too many times, he or she may exhaust the time limits for financial aid, or fail to meet the academic standards for eligibility.

Every school has its own Satisfactory Academic Process (SAP) policy which incorporates the Federal Student Assistance Satisfactory Academic Process standard. The school's financial aid office is responsible for keeping records and evaluating each student's academic progress every semester. The school's SAP standards for its own scholarship programs, grants, and state financial aid may differ from the federal standards. A good academic advisor will help the student stay on track and warn against decisions that might jeopardize financial aid status.

Three types of monitoring are required for students to remain eligible for federal student financial aid:

Degree Status

To receive federal financial aid, a student must be enrolled in a degree program at the undergraduate or graduate level. Students receive federal and state financial aid must take courses that count towards their degree or certificate programs. At most schools, each student is assigned an academic advisor who approves class schedules and helps make sure the student completes the classes required for the degree program. Federal regulations require that students have a GPA of at least "C" or its equivalent by the end of their second year of enrollment, or meet the school's academic standard of its degree program.

Time-to-Degree Limits

As of 2011, to remain eligible for financial aid, students must complete their degrees or certificates within a maximum time limit of 150 percent of the number of semesters or credit hours required for their primary degree program. The length of each degree program is determined by the school and published in its syllabus. Once that time frame has been exceeded, the student is no longer eligible for certain types of loans and financial aid. The school will notify a student when the end of that time farm is approaching The student can appeal to have the time extended if he or she has changed to a longer program of study. The semesters or credit hours completed under a previous program of study count as part of the new program hours.

NOTE: Barely half of all students complete a degree in six years.

A "Pathways to Prosperity" study by the Harvard Graduate School of Education in 2011 found that only 56 percent of the students who enter U.S. colleges and universities graduate within 6 years, and only 29 percent of students who enter 2-year programs complete their degrees within 3 years. According to a 2011 report from the National Center for Education Statistics, 78 percent of attendees at 4-year private for-profit schools fail to get a diploma after 6 years, compared to 35 percent of the students in non[profit private schools and 45 percent of the students in public colleges. Many of these students drop out of school because the academic work is too rigorous or because they have difficulty balancing the demands of classes with jobs and family responsibilities.

Completion Rate of Attempted Courses and Earned Credits

Federal regulations require a student to complete (earn) a minimum of 67 percent of the credits her or she "attempts" to remain eligible for student financial aid. Attempted credits include all credits for classes in which a student is formally enrolled on the first day of school,; credits for all the classes a student drops or adds, withdraws from, or fails during a semester; transfer credits from other universities that are accepted by the current school; and class credits attempted by taking an exam or submitting a portfolio. Earned credits include all classes for which a student receives a grade of "D" or better, Satisfactory, or Pass grades; transfer credits from another school that are accepted by the current institution; and credits earned by passing an exam or portfolio assessment.

Cumulative attempted and earned credits are tallied at the end of each semester. The completion rate is calculated by dividing the number of earned credits by the number of attempted credits. A low completion rate can result from failing grades, or from dropping or withdrawing from too many classes.

An undergraduate whose completion rate drops below 67 percent is given 1 probationary semester, during which he or she continues to receive financial aid, to bring the completion rate back up. A student failing to meet the 67 percent completion requirement at the end of the probationary semester will be denied financial aid in future semesters until his or her completion rate is back up to 67 percent or more. Only 1 financial aid warning semester is allowed. Graduate students do not receive a probationary semester. Their financial aid is immediately withdrawn, and they must bring their completion rate back up to 67 percent before they can again qualify to receive financial aid.

Federal Financial Aid

The U.S. government sponsors a variety of financial aid programs developed over the years to encourage students to pursue higher education.

As of the 2013-2014 academic year, the federal government offered these student financial aid programs:

Federal Pell Grant
Federal Supplemental Educational Opportunity Grant (FSEOG or SEOG)
Federal Work Study
Federal Perkins Loan
Subsidized and Unsubsidized Federal Direct Loans (also known as Stafford Loans)
Federal Parent Loan for Undergraduate Students (PLUS)
Federal Graduate PLUS Loan for graduate and professional degree students
Teacher Education Assistance for College and Higher Education Grant Program (TEACH)
Iraq and Afghanistan Service Grants

Some of these programs are open to all students regardless of their economic circumstances. Need-based financial aid is available only to students from lower-income families, and is intended to help academically talented students who could not otherwise afford a college education.

> **NOTE**: As college costs continue to rise, students are finding it increasingly difficult to make ends meet. Federal student loan limits are not keeping up with increases in tuition and living expenses. Eligibility for the Pell Grant has been limited to six years, and the maximum amount of the Pell Grant was reduced by $564 for the 2013-2014 school year. As a result, many students from low-income families are forced to drop out of school because they have no other financial resources.

Need-Based Financial Aid

A student's eligibility for need-based financial aid, and the amount of aid awarded, is determined by the school using information from the student's Free Application for Federal Student Aid (FAFSA) and a complex formula that attempts to balance college costs with a student's ability to pay. The formula is used to calculate a student's Expected Family Contribution (EFC), the amount the family is expected to pay for one year of college. The EFC is based on factors such as family income, certain investment assets, the number of people in the household, and the number of family members attending college. Students with lower EFCs qualify for need-based financial aid.

Even if you think you will not qualify for need-based financial aid, you should always fill out a FAFSA. For the 2007-2008 school year, 4.1 percent of Pell Grant recipients had a family AGI of more than $50,000. (Most families that are eligible for Pell Grants have incomes that average less than $25,000 per year.) Your EFC may change from year to year. For example, if a second member of your family starts college, your EFC will be halved because it will be divided between two students. Colleges and universities also use the EFC to select recipients for other types of grants and scholarships.

Some need-based financial aid, such as the Pell Grant, is guaranteed to eligible students. Other financial aid awards, like the FSEOG and Federal Work Study, depend on the amount of funds a particular school has available for that academic year.

It is essential that the student and the student's family fill out the FAFSA early every year in order to remain eligible for federal financial aid. If the family's income status changes during the academic year, the student can ask the school to reassess his or her eligibility for need-based financial aid. For example, if a parent dies, loses a job, or becomes incapacitated, the family should contact the financial aid office with a revised estimate of its income for the year. The student will be required to provide documentation, such as a severance letter or medical report. The reverse is also true. Part of the student loan contract is an agreement to notify the financial aid office of any significant change in family income. If a parent accepts a lucrative job offer, wins the lottery, or receives a large financial settlement, the school should be informed.

Federal Pell Grant

Named after the late U.S. Senator Claiborne Pell (D-RI), the Federal Pell Grant Program provides need-based grants to low-income undergraduate and to certain students rolled in a graduate teacher certification program. A Federal Pell Grant does not have to be repaid. Approximately 5,400 schools participate in the program. Since 1973 more than 60 million students have benefited from Pell Grants. Between 2008 and 2010, the number of students receiving Pell Grants almost doubled due to the recession. In 2012, the federal government disbursed $34.5 billion to more than 9 million students.

When the Pell grant program began in 1973, the maximum Pell Grant paid almost all of a student's tuition. Today, owing to the rapidly escalating cost of tuition, the maximum Pell Grant covers only about 21 percent of the cost of attending a post-secondary school.

NOTE: Students may not receive federal Pell Grant funds from more than one school at a time.

For the 2013–14 award year (July 1, 2013 to June 30, 2014), the annual Federal Pell Grant award ranged from a minimum of $582 to a maximum of $5,645. A student's eligibility and the amount the school awards is based on your family income and EFC, the cost of attendance (COA) as determined by the institution, whether the student is enrolled full-time or part-time, and whether the student attends for a full academic year or less. The annual amount may change from year to year. Approximately half of Pell grant recipients have family Adjusted Gross Incomes (AGI) family incomes of $15,000 or less. The families of about one fourth of Pell Grant own a home or pay a mortgage.

Until 2012, the Pell grant was available for up to 18 semesters. Now a student can receive the Federal Pell Grant for only 12 semesters, and it is no longer available during summer semesters.

> **NOTE**: If your parent died in military service in Iraq or Afghanistan while you were younger than 24 or enrolled in college, and you are eligible to receive a Federal Pell Grant, your EFC will be reduced to zero so that you can get the maximum amount.

Federal Supplemental Educational Opportunity Grant (FSEOG)

Federal Supplemental Educational Opportunity Grant (FSEOG, or SEOG) program provides need-based grants to help low-income undergraduate students finance the costs of postsecondary education by supplementing other types of financial aid.

Approximately 3,800 schools participate in the FSEOG program. Every year these institutions submit a Fiscal Operations Report and Application to Participate (FISAP) to the U.S. Department of Education. Each school then receives a funding allocation based on prior years' funding levels and on the aggregate need of the previous year's eligible students. The school awards these grants to the students with the lowest EFCs, and those who are already receiving Pell grants.

To receive a SEOG, the student must fill out the FAFSA. Awards range from $100 to a maximum of $4,000 per academic year. The school determines how much the student receives. The amount awarded each year depends on the amount of funding available and the number of eligible undergraduates attending the school that year.

Federal Work Study

The Federal Work Study (FWS) Program helps eligible students earn money to pay for their education expenses by working part-time. The employer may be the institution itself; a federal, state, or local public agency; a private nonprofit organization; or a private for-profit organization. The FWS program is administered by the school or university.

Eligibility for FWS is need-based, and the student must indicate that he or she is interested in work-study when filling out the FAFSA. If your student is eligible, the amount of work-study available will be included in his or her financial aid award letter. The student is then responsible to apply for a work-study job. These jobs are usually advertised on the school website, through various academic departments, and in the school human resources office.

Undergraduate students are paid an hourly wage, but graduate students may receive a salary depending on the job. The hourly wage must not be lower than the federal minimum wage, and may be higher for jobs requiring special skills or experience. Students receive a paycheck at least once a month, and are paid directly unless they request that the money be applied to tuition or other school fees. A student cannot earn more than the amount of FWS awarded each semester.

In contrast to ordinary part-time jobs in retail or food service, work-study jobs offer flexible hours that accommodate a student's class schedule. The student's academic progress has priority. Most work-study jobs give students time off to study before final exams, and time off during school holidays. Each school has its own regulations, but generally the job cannot exceed 12 hours per week.

Work-study is an excellent opportunity. Some of the jobs give students valuable work experience in their fields of interest, for example, working as a research assistant or lab technician, or in a library or museum. Many allow the student to interact with professors and other students and develop friendships and helpful contacts. Jobs are often conveniently located on or near the campus. A regular work schedule helps the student to manage time and maintain a study routine.

Federal work study awards range from $1,000 to as much as $4,000 per year.

Approximately 3,400 postsecondary institutions participate in the FWS program. Each institution applies annually for FWS funding by submitting a FISAP to the U.S. Department of Education. The Department uses a formula to allocate funds based on the institution's previous funding level and the aggregate need of eligible students in attendance in the prior year. In most cases, the school or the employer must pay up to a 50 percent share of a student's FWS wages. For some jobs, such as reading or mathematics tutors, the federal share of the wages can be as high as 100 percent. Institutions must use at least seven percent of their FWS allocations to support students working in community service jobs, such as tutoring preschoolers, elementary, and middle-school students in reading and math; family literacy projects; and emergency preparedness and response.

Since FWS funds are allocated on a first-come, first-serve basis, fill in the FAFSA as early as possible each year to let the school know you are interested. Once your student has been awarded work-study, he or she should start looking for a suitable job. A department or project might have funding for only one or two work-study positions, and the most desirable jobs are taken quickly.

Our two older daughters both benefited from work-study and gained friends and practical experience. One worked for the marine biology department, going out on boats to collect fish samples and learning to dissect them in the lab. Another worked in the human resources office, and later in a horticultural greenhouse on the university campus. The regular paycheck helped pay for food, supplies, and textbooks.

Our third daughter was not as fortunate. She attended a large university, and though she was awarded work-study, the recession had hit and the school FWS program was underfunded by $250,000. The jobs were available but the money was not. She eventually found a part-time job in a restaurant several miles from campus, often returning to her dorm late at night. She was not able to take extra time off to study for exams because her managers expected her to work a regular weekly schedule, and sometimes she could not come home for holidays. She had to pay an extra fee to stay in her dorm for part of the Christmas vacation because she was needed at her job. She learned from her work experience, but sometimes found that socializing with the other employees, who were not students, distracted her from school.

Perkins Loans

The Federal Perkins Loan Program originated with the National Defense Education Act in 1958 as the first federally sponsored low-interest student loan program. In 1986 it was given its present name to honor Carl D. Perkins, a former member of the U.S. House of Representatives from Kentucky who campaigned for student financial aid.

The Federal Perkins Loan Program gives need-based loans to students from low-income families. The school itself is the lender of a Perkins loan. Approximately 1,700 postsecondary institutions participate in the program. Schools replenish their Perkins loan funds by combining reimbursements from the Department of Education with money collected in payments from previous Perkins loan borrowers.

To receive a Perkins loan, a student must fill out the FAFSA. Perkins loans are given to students who have exceptional need for financial aid. The school determines which students are eligible for a Perkins loan based on their family income and the amount of funds available at the school. The maximum Perkins loans for undergraduates is $5,500 per year, with a maximum total of $27,500 for an undergraduate. For graduate students the maximum is $8,000 per year, with a lifetime limit of $60,000 including undergraduate Perkins loans. The school determines the amount each student will receive as part of his or her financial aid award package.

Perkins loans are similar to Federal Subsidized Student Loans, with some additional advantages. There is no interest until repayment begins, and no loan fee. The grace period is longer - nine months until you have to begin paying off the loan. Once repayment begins, the interest rate is fixed at 5 percent for the duration of the 10-year repayment period. Perkins Loans are eligible for full or partial Federal Loan Cancellation for borrowers who work in a variety of public service jobs, including teachers in designated low-income schools and designated teacher shortage areas such as math, science, and bilingual education; military service in a hostile fire or imminent danger area; Peace Corps and VISTA volunteers; full-time firefighters; corrections and law enforcement officers; attorneys who work as public defenders; and nurses and medical technicians.

Since Perkins loans are disbursed and managed by the schools, a borrower who has difficulty repaying a Perkins Loan should contact the school where he or she received the loan to ask about deferment or forbearance or to make payment arrangements.

Subsidized Direct Student Loans (Stafford Loans)

Subsidized Direct Student Loans (also known as Stafford Loans) are intended to help students from lower-income families go to college by lessening the long-term financial burden on the student. The U.S. government pays for the interest on Subsidized Direct Student Loans while the student is in school and during periods of deferment. This means that by the time the loan is paid off, the student will have paid less for his or her education than a student who received an Unsubsidized Direct Loan.

If you are enrolled in an income-based repayment Plan (IBR), and your monthly payment does not cover the interest that accrues on your loans each month, the government will also pay the unpaid accrued interest on your Direct Subsidized Loans or Subsidized Federal Stafford Loans for up to three consecutive years from the date you began repaying your loan under IBR.

Until July 1, 2012, the U.S. Government continued to pay the interest on Subsidized Direct Loans during the six-month grace period after the student leaves school. This benefit is no longer available; interest begins to accrue on the loan as soon as the student leaves school. If this interest is not paid by the end of the six-month grace period, it is added to the amount of the loan (capitalized) and increases the overall amount repaid by the student.

On July 1, 2012, the U.S. Government stopped offering Subsidized Direct Loans to graduate students. Students can still borrow Unsubsidized Direct Loans to pay for postgraduate studies.

NOTE: Loss of Subsidized Student Loan Benefits Hurts Graduate Students

The new Income-Based Repayment (IBR) program undermines the benefit of having the government pay your student loan interest while you are in school – having a lower amount to pay off. After you make payments of 10 percent of your disposable income for 20 years, any remaining loan balance is forgiven. The other benefits – having interest paid during periods of deferment, and when an IBR payment is not large enough to cover the interest – could mean a lot to graduate students who incur additional debt in order to advance their educational qualifications. Their debt will continue to increase during these periods.

Subsidized Direct Student Loans (also known as Stafford Loans) are available only to students from families with low EFCs. About 66 percent of Subsidized Direct Loans are awarded to students with family AGIs under $50,000, 25 percent to students with family AGIs between $50,000 and $100,000, and slightly less than 10 percent to students with family AGIs over $100,000.

The application process, interest rates, and repayment schedule are similar to Unsubsidized Direct Loans (see below). The first step is to fill out the FAFSA so your EFC can be calculated and the school can process your loan application.

There is a limit to how much the student can receive each academic year in subsidized loans:

> First year: $3,500
> Second year: $4,500
> Third and subsequent years: $5,500
> Total undergraduate limit: $23,000

The school determines exactly how much money will be awarded, based on the cost of attendance; the amount the student is receiving in scholarships, grants, and other financial aid programs; and the family EFC.

If your student is awarded an Unsubsidized Direct Student Loan, it is the best loan option available because of the low interest rate and the interest subsidy. If the student needs more than the subsidized loan amount, up to $2,000 in additional Unsubsidized Direct Student Loans may be added to the financial aid award.

NOTE: Federal Family Education Loan (FFEL) Program
As of July 1, 2010, the Federal Family Education Loan (FFEL) Program has been phased out. FFEL Program loans were made by private lenders such as banks, credit unions, and savings and loan associations. Existing FFEL loans will continue in repayment.

TEACH Grant

A *Teacher Education Assistance for College and Higher Education (TEACH) Grant* provides up to $4,000 per year (reduced to $3,760 by the sequestration of 2013) to students who intend to make a career of teaching. It is a loan that does not have to be paid back as long as you work for at least four years within eight years of finishing your program as a highly qualified (certified), full-time secondary or elementary teacher in a high-need subject area at a school serving low income students.

To receive a TEACH Grant you must qualify for federal financial aid (see *How to Qualify for Financial Aid* above) and be enrolled in a program that is eligible for the TEACH Grant at a participating school. Not all schools offer TEACH Grants, and a program that qualifies for the TEACH Grant at one school may not qualify at another. If you are interested in the TEACH Grant, inquire about eligible programs at your school's financial aid office.

Each year that you receive a TEACH Grant, you must receive TEACH Grant counseling and sign an Agreement to Serve on the TEACH Grant website accepting the terms and conditions for receiving a TEACH Grant. You must also meet certain academic achievement requirements (generally, scoring above the 75th percentile on one or more portions of a college admissions test or maintaining a cumulative GPA of at least 3.25).

The U.S. Department of Education determines which subject areas are high-need and maintains a list of schools serving low-income students on its website (https://www.tcli.ed.gov/CBSWebApp/tcli/).

You should not accept a TEACH Grant if you are not committed to a teaching career. If you fail to complete the four years of service within eight years of completing your program, the TEACH Grant will convert to a Federal Direct Unsubsidized Loan with interest accrued from the date of the first disbursal of the funds. You will have a six-month grace period before you must begin making loan payments. **Once the grant converts to a loan, it cannot be converted back to a grant.** You can request an extension of the eight-year service period under certain circumstances such as medical leave or service as a military reservist. If you pass away or become totally disabled without completing the teaching requirement, the debt will be forgiven.

State Government Student Loans

In addition to Federal Direct Student Loans, your student may be eligible for student loans guaranteed by the government of the state where the student goes to school. Some states also offer assistance in applying for and receiving federal student loans, for example, paying the one percent origination fee so that students receive the full loan amount.

Like federal loans, state government loans offer lower interest rates and flexible repayment options. Not all states offer student loans, and the amounts and eligibility requirements are set by state legislators. Your school or university financial aid office has information on the availability of state loans and will include these in your financial aid package.

Some examples of state government student loans include:

ALASKA: The Alaska Commission on Postsecondary Education offers an Alaska Supplementary Education Loan (ASEL) as well as career-specific loans that may be forgiven if the student works in areas of Alaska where there are shortages of professionals.

DELAWARE: The Higher Education Office of the Delaware Department of Education offers a variety of Professional Incentive Loans for students in fields such as nursing, teaching, medicine, and veterinary medicine. Loan forgiveness is available, generally at a rate of one year of loan forgiveness for each year of service in Delaware after graduation.

MINNESOTA: The Minnesota Office of Higher Education administers the SELF loan program, through which undergraduate and graduate students can borrow up to $10,000 per year.

Unsubsidized Direct Student Loans

Unsubsidized Direct student loans are available to any student, regardless of family income. Direct student loans offer a fixed interest rate, making it possible for the student to have consistent monthly payments over the ten-year repayment period.

There is a limit to how much the student can receive each academic year in Direct student loans:

> First year: $5,500
> Second year: $6,500
> Third and subsequent years: $7,500
> Total undergraduate limit: $31,000

If the student is also receiving a Subsidized Direct student loan, that amount is included in the limit; a freshman receiving the maximum $3,500 in Subsidized Direct Loans can receive only an additional $2,000 in Unsubsidized Direct loans. The school determines how much money the student actually receives, based on its cost of attendance (COA).

To apply for a Direct Loan, the student and family must complete and submit the FAFSA. The school uses information from the FAFSA to calculate your EFC and determine how much loan money you are eligible to receive. You are not eligible to receive more than the COA, minus your EFC and the amount of any scholarships and grants.

A student who has borrowed the maximum amount and then paid off part of the loan can borrow again, up to the eligible limit.

Direct Loans are included in your student's award letter as part of his or her financial aid package.

There is a 1 percent loan origination fee on all Direct Subsidized Loans and Direct Unsubsidized Loans. This loan fee is deducted from each loan disbursement.

Interest on an Unsubsidized Direct Student Loan accrues during the time that the student is enrolled in school more than half-time, and during the six-month grace period before the student must begin repaying the loan. You can significantly reduce the amount that must be repaid by making regular interest payments while the student is still in school. You can also pay the accrued interest during the grace period, before the loan goes into repayment. Once repayment begins, any remaining accrued interest is capitalized - added to the loan principal. From that time on, interest is charged on the principal plus the accrued interest, increasing the amount of the monthly payment and adding thousands to the amount that must be paid off.

Independent Students

The Unsubsidized Direct Student Loan aggregate limit is higher for independent students. It is assumed that an independent student will not be receiving any support from his or her parents in paying for an education. Not living with parents or not being claimed by them on tax forms does not make you an independent student for purposes of applying for federal student aid.

An independent student is one of the following:
- At least 24 years old
- Married
- A graduate or professional student
- A veteran
- A member of the armed forces
- An orphan or a ward of the court
- Someone with dependent children or legal dependents other than a spouse
- An emancipated minor
- Someone who is homeless or at risk of becoming homeless

> **NOTE**: The definition of a veteran does *not* include:
> - Someone who has never engaged in active duty in the U.S. armed forces
> - A current Reserve Officers' Training Corps (ROTC) student
> - A cadet or midshipman at a service academy
> - A National Guard or Reserves enlistee activated only for state or training purposes
> - Someone who was dishonorably discharged from active duty in the U.S. armed forces
> - Someone currently serving in the U.S. armed forces who will continue to serve through June 30 of the year for which he or she is filling out a FAFSA

Your status as an independent student will be determined based on your answers to questions in the FAFSA.

The annual Direct Student Loan limits for independent students are:

First year: $9,500
Second year: $10,500
Third and subsequent years: $12,500
Total undergraduate limit: $57,000

Professional or graduate students: $20,500
Total graduate limit: $138,500 (This includes all loans received as an undergraduate.)

These limits include any amounts received as Subsidized Direct Student Loans. A sophomore receiving the maximum $4,500 in Subsidized Direct Loans can receive no more than an additional $6,000 in Unsubsidized Direct Loans.

Beginning July 1, 2012, graduate and professional students are no longer eligible for Subsidized Direct Student Loans. Graduate and professional students enrolled in certain health profession programs may be eligible to receive additional Direct Unsubsidized Loan amounts each academic year. For these students, there is also a higher aggregate limit. If you are enrolled in a health profession program, consult the *financial aid office* at your school for information about annual and aggregate limits.

Dependent students whose parents do not qualify for a Parent PLUS Loan are also eligible for higher loan limits. A parent might not qualify for a PLUS loan if:

- The parent has a bad credit history.
- The parent is incarcerated.
- The parent's whereabouts are unknown.
- The parent has declared bankruptcy and cannot incur additional debt.
- The parent can demonstrate an inability to repay the loan because of low income.
- The parent is not an eligible borrower for other reasons, such as not being a U.S. citizen or a permanent resident of the U.S.

To apply for a Parent PLUS loan, the parent or student must fill out a FAFSA. Once a parent has been denied a Parent PLUS loan, the denial is good for the entire academic year. If a parent is later approved for a PLUS loan before all the loan funds have been disbursed for the academic year, the student may be returned to a dependent status with lower Unsubsidized Direct Loan limits.

A student whose parents do not qualify for a Parent PLUS loan might be eligible for larger Unsubsidized Direct loans, and should consult the financial aid office at his or her school.

> **NOTE: Talk to a financial aid advisor**
> Before you apply for a Parent PLUS loan, your student should talk to a financial aid advisor about your family's exceptional circumstances. The financial aid official might determine that your student qualifies for additional Unsubsidized Direct Student loans. You might think your low income or poor credit score will disqualify you for a Parent PLUS loan, but that is sometimes not the case. Once you apply for the Parent PLUS loan and are accepted, your student will no longer be eligible for increased Unsubsidized Direct Student loans that year. (A parent's refusal to borrow a PLUS loan is not considered an exceptional circumstance.)

Direct PLUS loans

Direct PLUS loans are federal loans to graduate or professional degree students and parents of dependent undergraduate students to help pay education expenses. The lender is the federal government and the loans are available through schools participating in the Direct Loan program.

To obtain a Direct PLUS loan, you must be eligible to receive federal financial aid and, if you are borrowing on behalf of your child, your child must also be eligible.

To apply for a Direct PLUS loan, fill out the FAFSA and follow your school's procedure for requesting the loan. You will then undergo a credit check. If you have an adverse credit history, you can still qualify for the loan by obtaining a credit-worthy cosigner. The student for whom you are borrowing the loan cannot be your cosigner.

You will then be required to sign a Master Promissory Note (MPN), agreeing to the terms of the loan. Graduate or professional students must complete entrance counseling through their schools before receiving a PLUS loan.

The amount of the loan will be the school's COA minus any other loans, grants or scholarships.

A 4.204% loan origination fee will be proportionately deducted from each Direct PLUS loan disbursement.

For graduate or professional students, a Direct PLUS loan is placed into *deferment* while the student is enrolled at least half-time and for an additional six months after the student ceases to be enrolled at least half-time. Parent PLUS loans go into repayment as soon as they are disbursed, but the parent can contact the loan servicer to request deferment while the child is enrolled at least half-time and for a six-month grace period after the child leaves school.

A Direct PLUS Loan made to a parent cannot be transferred to the child after graduation. The parent is responsible for repaying the loan. Repayment options are similar to those available for Unsubsidized Direct Loans.

NOTE: Consider the advantages of a Parent PLUS loan before taking out private student loans.
Some parents are reluctant to take out a Parent PLUS loan because the financial obligation to pay back the loan cannot be transferred to the student later on. Instead, they prefer to cosign a private student loan with an option that allows the cosigner to be released after a certain number of payments have been made. Before borrowing a private loan, compare the interest rates, fees, and repayment options carefully. The fixed low interest rates make Parent PLUS loans a good option, if you can make a private agreement with your student that he or she will take responsibility for paying back the loan later on.

Fees

A loan origination fee of 1.051 percent for Direct Subsidized Loans and Direct Unsubsidized Loans and 4.204 percent for Direct PLUS Loans is deducted from each student loan disbursement. These fees are included in the amount of loan principal that you must repay. There is no loan origination fee for Perkins Loans because the federal government covers administration costs.

Some private loans include origination fees or fees when the loan enters repayment; other private loans advertise no fees but compensate with higher interest rates.

Entrance Counseling

Students receiving their first federal Direct Subsidized or Direct Unsubsidized loans and graduate students taking out their first Direct PLUS loan must complete entrance counseling before the school can disburse their loans. Parents taking out a Direct PLUS loan for a child's education do not need to complete entrance counseling.

The entrance counseling may be conducted in person by a financial aid officer at the school, or the school might provide you with the URL for its online counseling session. The school might also direct you to complete the 30-minute online counseling at Studentloans.gov (https://studentloans.gov/myDirectLoan/counselingInstructions.action).

The entrance counseling explains what a Direct loan is and how the loan process works. You are informed of your rights and responsibilities as a student borrower, educated about managing your education expenses, and told about other ways to finance your education.

Complete your entrance counseling as early as possible. Your loan will not be disbursed until this requirement is met.

Your Master Promissory Note

Before a federal student loan is disbursed, the student must sign a Master Promissory Note (MPN). The Master Promissory Note is the legal contract spelling out all the conditions of the loan and the obligations of the borrower. The Master Promissory Note for federal student loans can be filled out and signed electronically on the Federal Student Aid website (https://studentloans.gov/myDirectLoan/whatYouNeed.action?page=mpn). You can also sign a paper MPN at your school financial aid office. After you have signed a federal Master Promissory Note for your first student loan, it will be kept on file and automatically applied to all your subsequent federal student loans for up to 10 years.

Some schools require students to sign an MPN each academic year. If you sign an MPN and the loan is not disbursed within one year, you will have to sign a new one. A parent or a graduate student taking out a Direct PLUS loan must also sign a Master Promissory Note. A parent taking out loans for more than one student must sign a separate MPN for each student. A borrower of Direct PLUS loans also has to sign a new MPN if a cosigner is added because of bad credit.

To sign your MPN you will need to enter your personal information, contact information for three references, and your federal student aid PIN. Parents signing MPNs must use their own PINs. As part of the submission process, you are asked to affirm that you have read and understood the terms of the MPN. You may be tempted to quickly skim over the MPN and click the check box, but take the time to read each section. The MPN contains important information about the borrower's legal obligations.

Soon after you have submitted a signed MPN, you will receive a financial disclosure statement of the loans your school will be disbursing under the MPN, including the loan amount, fees, and the expected disbursement dates and amounts. Many schools also mail you a printed copy of the MPN. You can look up your MPN online anytime by signing in to "Manage My Direct Loans" on the StudentLoans.gov home page.

The Master Promissory Note contains detailed information about your student loans, including how interest is calculated, the amounts of loan origination fees, and the day your grace period ends. Keep a printed copy of your MPN on file for reference. Most of your questions about federal student loans are answered somewhere in the language of the MPN.

The terms of a MPN are legally binding, just like any other legal contract. Violating these terms could result in the loss of future access to federal student loans, and the student could be asked to pay the loan money back right away. For example, under the MPN Terms and Conditions, your federal student loan could become "immediately due and payable" if you spend the money for anything except authorized education expenses at the school that certified your eligibility for the loan. Authorized education expenses are defined as:

- Tuition
- Room
- Board
- Institutional fees
- Books
- Supplies
- Equipment
- Dependent child care expenses
- Transportation
- Commuting expenses
- Rental or purchase of a personal computer
- Loan fees
- Other documented, authorized costs

NOTE: The terms of the MPN are legally binding.
The school is not likely to ask every student borrower for receipts documenting how loan money has been spent, but it would be a violation of the MPN to use student loan money for other purposes such as investing in the stock market, starting a business, or paying off unrelated credit card debt. Signing the MPN is an admission that you are aware of these restrictions on the use of student loan money; you cannot claim later on that you did not know about the consequences.

In another section of the MPN, you agree to notify the school financial aid office, and later on, your loan servicer, whenever your contact information changes, your employment status changes, or you change employers. The MPN also describes how you will receive important notices about your loans (by email or by letters sent to your home address). You cannot say you never received these notices if they were sent to the addresses listed in your loan documents.

Disbursement

You will first learn about your federal and state student loan offers from your school's award letter. The award letter should indicate how much you are receiving in subsidized and unsubsidized loans.

You must officially accept the loans by following the school's acceptance procedure. Most schools allow you to do this online. If you are unable to accept the loans through the school's financial aid website, you should visit the financial aid office to sign the documents. A phone conversation or email is not considered an official acceptance notice. You are also required to specify how you want the loan to be disbursed. You can specify whether you want the loan money to be applied only to your school bills, or whether you want the remaining amount disbursed to you as cash. You must also authorize the school to make a direct deposit to your bank account, or send you a paper check. If you change your mind about any of these things, you must officially inform the school through its online process or in writing. Only the person responsible for repaying the loan (your student, or you if you are borrowing a Parent PLUS loan) can accept the loan and authorize payments.

A portion of the loan is disbursed each semester or academic period. When you indicate that you have accepted the loans, the school first applies your loan funds to your school account to pay for tuition, fees, housing, food plans, outstanding charges from previous years, and other school charges. If you have authorized it, any amount left over is disbursed to the student through a check mailed to the student or a direct deposit into the student's bank account.

Student loan money is typically disbursed to the student during the first days of each semester. After the loan is disbursed, the student will receive notice from the school, either electronically or in a letter. A student who does not receive a disbursement when expected should check the school's financial aid website or visit the financial aid office. Sometimes a disbursement is delayed because the student has failed to complete the loan acceptance process, or because bank information is incorrect.

The amount disbursed might not match the amount on the award letter exactly because a loan origination fee is deducted from each disbursement.

Many schools hold back disbursement of leftover student loan money 30 days the first semester for incoming freshmen. This protects the student from incurring unnecessary debt in case he or she decides not to stay at the school. Since most freshmen are housed on campus with mandatory food plans, their basic needs will be met during this period. Most schools also offer financial aid recipients and student loan borrowers an advance credit of $600 at the campus bookstore so that students can purchase textbooks and supplies before classes begin. Be prepared with some spending money so your student can buy school and dormitory supplies when he or she first arrives at school.

NOTE: Clear up any misunderstandings.
If there is any doubt or confusion about student loan money, encourage your student to talk to a financial aid official right away and clear up misunderstandings. A student has enough anxiety about classes and academic decisions without having to worry about whether he or she will be able to pay for school expenses. The problem may be a simple miscommunication. The student might not have completed the loan acceptance procedure, or might need to apply for additional funds. Many schools offer temporary emergency loans to carry students over until financial aid is disbursed.

Soon after a loan is disbursed, you will receive a letter or notice from your loan servicer stating the amount that has been disbursed and giving other details about the loan. You will receive updates for the loan servicer at regular intervals, including statements of the interest that has accrued so that you can pay it off while your student is still in school if you want to. You can look up your student loan statements at any time on the loan servicer's website.

Cancellation

Before a student loan is disbursed, you can cancel the loan, or part of it, by notifying the school. After the loan is disbursed, you can return the money and cancel all or part of your loan without penalty within the time frames set out in the Master Promissory Note. A school is required to cancel the loan if you notify it in writing (or electronically) within 14 days after disbursement. After 14 days, you must follow the school's cancellation policy. If cancellation is no longer an option, you can repay the loan to the loan servicer without penalty.

Use of Student Loan Money

When a student signs the Master Promissory Note, he or she agrees to use financial aid and student loan money only for education expenses. This can be loosely interpreted to include some personal expenses. Many students spend loan money for clothing, items to decorate their dorm rooms, travel, and eating out. Parents should emphasize that this money should not be used for luxuries or major purchases, such as a used car or a flat-screen TV. A sudden influx of cash into your bank account can be exhilarating, but students need to know that they will be paying this money back, with interest, for decades to come. The money also has to last for the entire semester.

A student who does not need all the student loan money that has been disbursed should either return some of it to lower the loan principal, or save it for the next semester's expenses. When a student moves into off-campus housing he or she will need to pay a security deposit and the first month's rent, often several weeks before financial aid is disbursed. If possible, try to keep some financial aid money from the previous semester for this purpose. Extra money can also be kept to buy textbooks online in advance for the next semester's classes.

> **NOTE: Help your student develop a financial plan.**
> Your student might or might not have acquired financial wisdom during high school. Feeling generous, with money in the bank, students have been known to use student loan money to treat all their friends to dinner, buy lavish birthday gifts for a girlfriend or boyfriend, or bring home expensive Christmas presents for everyone in the family. Knowing that your student has cash, friends may ask for loans or just leave him or her to pay the utility bills for a shared apartment. If you know your child cannot say no, have a discussion about money management and develop a strategy to control spending wisely.

Though schools do not generally police the ways in which students spend the student loan money disbursed to them, it is a violation of the student loan contract (set forth in the Master Promissory Note) to use student loan money for purposes other than education. Technically, if a student is caught misusing student loan funds, the loan could be canceled and the money would have to be immediately repaid.

Your Student's Award Letter

Based on the information in the student and family FAFSAs, your school puts together a financial aid package that includes federal and state need-based scholarships and grants (if your student is eligible), scholarships and grants offered directly by the school, federal work-study, and subsidized and unsubsidized federal and state loans.

This information is provided to you online or through the mail in an award letter soon after you receive an acceptance letter from the school (usually early March or late April). The name "award letter" is deceptive, because the letter typically combines offers of free money (scholarships, waivers, and grants) with loans, which you will pay back with interest, and work-study, which must be earned by working at a job.

There is no universal format for award letters. Each school presents the information differently, and the names and codes assigned to various items can be confusing. The award letter is very important, though, because it tells you how much money you will need for the school year, how much you will receive in grants and scholarships, and how much you will be able to borrow in federal student loans. If you do not understand the information in the award letter, contact the financial aid office or speak to a financial aid officer during a campus tour or student orientation.

The school determines the amount of financial aid available to a student by subtracting the EFC (from the FAFSA) from the school's Cost Of Attendance (COA). Each school calculates its own COA. The COA must include tuition, room and board, and books and supplies. The school can add other costs at its discretion, such as student health insurance, travel and transportation, dependent child care, the cost of a computer, and an amount for personal expenses. Schools often underestimate these discretional costs in their COAs to make themselves seem less expensive. A detailed breakdown of the school's COA can be found on the school's website or in its catalog. Your actual costs could be higher or lower depending on your personal circumstances. For example, if your student is living at home, you will not need to pay for room and board. You do not need to pay for health insurance if your student is covered by your own policy. If the school is out-of-state, add the cost of traveling to and from school.

Every student qualifies for Unsubsidized Direct student loans regardless of need. Most schools include them in the award letter to demonstrate how the student can use them to pay for education and to make families aware that they are available. Some award letters also include private loans from the school's "preferred lender." (You are not obligated to get a private loan through the school and might find better terms from another lender.)

Some schools require the student to formally accept or decline each form of financial aid in the award letter; others do not. To receive student loans you must go through the acceptance process, including entrance counseling. You can decline student loans, or accept only a portion of the amount offered. Declining the student loans does not increase the amount of need-based aid you are awarded.

The amount of Subsidized Direct student loans offered in the award letter is based on the information in your FAFSA. If you believe you are eligible for additional amounts, meet with the financial aid official to explain your family's exceptional circumstances.

The loans in your award letter might be difficult to distinguish from need-based financial aid. Look for the letters LN next to the item; words like "Direct", "PLUS", "subsidized", and "unsubsidized"; and for the names of state student loan programs. The award letter typically does not include detailed information about these loans, such as interest rates and origination fees, making it difficult to calculate exactly how much they will cost. Use the information and the loan calculators on the Federal Student Aid website (www.direct.ed.gov/calc.html) to estimate how much you will pay in interest for federal student loans over the repayment period.

Award letters are issued every academic year. Your student might not receive the same amount of financial aid every year. Changes in family and student income and assets, and alterations in family circumstances, such as the number of dependents and number of students in college, will affect your EFC. Many schools offer more grants to incoming freshmen than they do in later years, so that larger loans are needed to make up the difference. The school's COA is likely to increase every year. Your student will probably graduate with a total student loan debt that is at least five times what he or she borrowed for freshman year.

When comparing award letters from two or more schools, consider all the factors:

- Look at each school's COA and calculate how much it will really cost your student to attend each school. Include extra expenses such as transportation to and from that school, housing, and clothing (such warm clothes for a colder climate).

- Look at how much "free money" each school is offering - scholarships, tuition and housing waivers, and grants that do not have to be repaid. A school with a high COA could cost you less than a cheaper school if your student receives enough grants and scholarship money. Find out if your student will receive the same amount each year. If the award letter includes work study, call the financial aid office to find out if jobs will be available for your student at the school.

- Finally, look at value for money. What kind of experience does each school offer? What are the campuses and dorms like? What are typical class sizes? Do any of the schools have special programs that fit your student's interests? Research the school's graduation rate and first-year retention rate. A high first-year retention rate indicates that the school has programs and policies that help freshmen adjust to academic life and succeed in their classes. Does the school help graduates to find jobs in their fields? Does your student have a preference?

An Award Letter Comparison Tool on Finaid.org can help you accurately compare two or more award letters (www.finaid.org/calculators/awardletter.phtml).

Following are three sample award letters for the same student for the 2009 - 2010 academic year. Note the differences in the total estimated cost for one year. This student is a Florida resident and will be paying out-of-state tuition at University of Northern Arizona and George Mason University. Each of these schools offers a $6,000 grant to compensate.

UF|UNIVERSITY *of* FLORIDA

Division of Student Affairs
Office for Student Financial Affairs

S-107 Criser Hall
P.O. Box 114025
Gainesville, Florida 32611-4025
(352) 392-1275
(352) 392-2861 Fax
http://www.sfa.ufl.edu/

Mar 24, 2009

UFID:

2009-2010 Award Letter

Below is a listing of your 2009-2010 financial aid awards as of the date of this notification.

Awards listed under Award Detail as "predicted" are only projections of what you are eligible to receive. Final determination of your eligibility and the award amount is based on information from the state of Florida, a private donor, a college or division within the University of Florida or the results of the financial aid application (FAFSA).

If you continue to meet all eligibility criteria, associated with each fund, awards will be disbursed each term as indicated below. For additional information please refer to the Award Letter Guide located on UF's ISIS Web site at www.isis.ufl.edu. Under "Financial Aid" select "Awards and Disbursements" under 2009-10.

Estimated cost of attendance from 08/28/2009 to 05/03/2010 . . . . $ 16744.00

Minus:
   Expected Parental Contribution 0.00
   Expected Student/Spouse Contribution 40.00

Equals your gross financial need . . . . $ 16704.00

Award Detail

	Fall	Spring	Summer A	Summer B	Total
PREDICTED FEDERAL PELL GRANT	2650.00	2650.00			5300.00
FEDERAL WORK STUDY	1500.00	1500.00			3000.00
PREDICTED FED DIRECT SUB LOAN	1722.00	1722.00			3444.00
PREDICTED FL ACADEMIC SCHOLAR	2078.00	2078.00			4156.00
PREDICTED FED ACAD COMP GRANT	375.00	375.00			750.00

Total Award . . . .$ 16650.00

1. If you are receiving aid from sources not listed, report them on UF's ISIS Web site at www.isis.ufl.edu. Under "Financial Aid" select "Additional Aid Reporting" under 2009-10.

2. To reduce or cancel any award, go to UF's ISIS Web site at www.isis.ufl.edu. Under "Financial Aid" select "Awards and Disbursements" under 2009-10.

3. If the total amount of your aid exceeds your gross financial need as a result of your receiving additional outside aid such as a scholarship or fellowship or due to a change in your expected family contribution, your need is considered overmet. If you receive funds that cause your need to be overmet, you may be required to repay the overmet amount. You will be notified if this occurs.

The Foundation for The Gator Nation
An Equal Opportunity Institution

Office of Student Financial Aid
4400 University Drive, 3B5
Fairfax, Virginia 22030
703-993-2353

Notice of Financial Aid Award and Acceptance
2009-2010 Aid Year

INSTRUCTIONS FOR COMPLETING
YOUR NOTICE OF AWARD

Indicated below are the results of our review or your application for financial assistance. In order to complete this form accurately and avoid possible complications **you must follow all of the steps outlined:**

1. **Read and Review** all award information and messages carefully.
2. **Enter either "Accept" or "Decline"** for each award in the response column. If you do not enter a response for an award, we will assume that you are declining the offer and the award will be cancelled.
3. **Sign and Date** the acknowledgement at the bottom of the enclosed Conditions of Award form.
4. **Return** one completed copy of the Notice of Award and one completed copy of the Conditions of Award form to our office within four weeks of the date printed on this letter. Other copies should be retained for your records.

April 2, 2009

This Financial Aid Award has been prepared for   Maeda   Student ID:

Accept/Decline	Description of Awards	Fall 2009	Spring 2010	Award Totals
_____	Federal Pell Grant	$2,650.00	$2,650.00	$5,300.00
_____	Fed Supp Ed Opp Grant	$600.00	$600.00	$1,200.00
_____	Federal Work-Study	$1,000.00	$1,000.00	$2,000.00
_____	Federal Perkins Loan	$1,000.00	$1,000.00	$2,000.00
_____	Fed Sub Stafford Loan	$1,750.00	$1,750.00	$3,500.00
_____	Fed Unsub Stafford Loan	$1,000.00	$1,000.00	$2,000.00
_____	Mason Out of State Grant	$3,000.00	$3,000.00	$6,000.00
	Totals:	$11,000.00	$11,000.00	$22,000.00

Award Messages

George Mason University is pleased to assist you in financing your education. Financial aid offered is considered to be supplemental to the resources of your family, yourself and other resources. The awards listed above are based on full time enrollment and the housing status you reported on your FAFSA. Financial aid awards may be reduced due to changes in housing, enrollment, residency or receipt of scholarships or other resources.

* * Grant awards: A grant award does not need to be repaid. Grants MAY be reduced due to changes in housing, hours and/or residency.

* * O/S GMU Grant: Award based on financial need, out of state residency and full time enrollment each semester. You must meet the following conditions to be considered for the O/S GMU Grant in future years:
1. Meet the March 1st financial aid priority filing date.
2. Continue to be degree-seeking.
3. Continue to meet the level of demonstrated need prescribed by the aid office.
4. Maintain financial aid satifactory progress standards.
5. Maintain out of state residency.
6. Maintain full-time (at least 12 credits) enrollment each semester.

* * Federal Stafford Loan: If you wish to borrow less money, simply reduce the award amount offered to you. Please note the award amounts each semester must be equal to begin your loan process. This loan amount is based on full-time enrollment and the housing status you reported on your FAFSA, your award may be adjusted and a notice will be sent to you.

You will be mailed information about completing a Federal Stafford Loan Master Promissory Note (MPN), if you have accepted the award. You will be able to complete this on-line using SallieMae's OpenNet website.

If you are a first time Federal Stafford Loan borrower, you will need to complete a loan entrance counseling session, which you can complete on-line at http://financialaid.gmu.edu or by visiting the office. The office is located in South Chesapeake Module on the Fairfax campus.

NORTHERN
ARIZONA
UNIVERSITY

03/17/2009

2009-2010
Financial Aid Award

Residency: Non-resident
Academic Level: Freshman
Enrollment:

Fall 2009   Full-Time
Spring 2010   Full-Time

ID Number:

Congratulations! We are pleased to offer you the following financial aid awards for 2009-2010:

	Fall 2009	Spring 2010	Total
Pres Scholarship Tuition Yr1	$1,875.00	$1,875.00	$3,750.00
Federal Pell Grant	$2,650.00	$2,650.00	$5,300.00
University Grant - NonRes	$3,080.00	$3,080.00	$6,160.00
Federal DL Sub Loan - AY	$1,750.00	$1,750.00	$3,500.00
Federal DL Unsub Loan - AY	$1,000.00	$1,000.00	$2,000.00
Federal PLUS Loan - Offered	$5,400.00	$5,400.00	$10,800.00
Total Financial Aid Offer	**$15,755.00**	**$15,755.00**	**$31,510.00**

Please refer to the award messages section in this letter for a detailed description of each award

Estimated Fall/Spring Costs

Direct Costs		Indirect Costs	
Tuition	$16,868.00	Transportation	$2,142.00
Student Activities Fees	$468.00	Miscellaneous	$3,244.00
Books and Supplies	$916.00	**Total**	**$5,386.00**
Housing	$4,344.00		
Meals	$3,528.00		
Total	**$26,124.00**		

Total Direct & Indirect Costs: $31,510.00

Summary of Financial Aid and Costs

Total Cost of Attendance	$31,510.00
Estimated Family Contribution	$ 40.00
Total Need	$31,470.00
Total Aid Offered	$31,510.00
Total Unmet Need	$ 0.00

Financial Aid and Scholarship Scams

During your child's junior year in high school you will probably begin receiving direct mail invitations to attend seminars or pay for official-sounding services that will help you find scholarships. You do not need to pay anyone for this type of assistance. This information is available for free. Your child will have more success finding scholarships through a high school guidance office, internet searches, and suggestions from the schools he or she is interested in. Your money is better invested in college application fees, SAT and ACT fees, or books and computer software that help prepare students for the SAT and ACT.

Mr. K:

We started prepaid tuition accounts for both of our sons when they were very young. Prepaid tuition is a good idea if your child is going to attend a state university. You pay the tuition rate that was in effect when you opened the account, and by the time your child is old enough for college, most of the tuition is taken care of. Of course, if your child decides to go to a private university or study out-of-state, your money is returned to you and you have to pay the current rate.

Our elder son just graduated from law school. When he started college, my employer offered scholarships for employees' children, and he qualified for the Florida Bright Futures scholarship, which was much more generous at that time. These scholarships, combined with the prepaid tuition and scholarships from his university, made it possible for him to get his undergraduate degree without incurring student loan debt. He worked his way through law school.

Our second son is now a sophomore at a private college, where he plays on the lacrosse team. When he was in high school, several out-of-state universities invited him to come and play on their lacrosse teams, but they did not offer him any scholarship money. Second and Third Division school don't offer athletic scholarships, and many First Division schools don't either.

Mr. K (cont'd):

Then I received a notice that my son qualified for an academic scholarship at a local private college, and I encouraged him to apply. He was accepted, and as it happened, the lacrosse coach from that college was guest speaker at my son's high school lacrosse banquet that year. My son won several awards that night, and the coach had seen him play, so he was invited to join the team.

Our son is aware that he must keep his grades up and maintain his academic scholarship if he wants to stay at this school. Student athletes have many demands placed on them. The lacrosse team has training from 6 am to 8 am and conditioning at 1 pm every day, plus a 2-hour study hall every night. During the lacrosse season, which runs from January to April, they often have to travel for away games. Last year, my son was in North Carolina the weekend before finals week. He had three papers due the day after he got back. Playing on the team helps to keep him focused, and many of his good friends are his teammates, but he has to work hard.

My wife attended Penn State and had the whole college experience. I started community college two years after high school and lived at home while attending college. I believe it is important for a student to live on campus and become wholly involved in campus life. Though our son could easily live at home and commute to school, we encouraged him to live in the dorms so he could make friends and become more independent.

We give our son a small weekly allowance so he can pay for his gas and social activities. I have encouraged him to apply for a job on campus, just a few hours a week, because on-campus employers understand a student's schedule. I am concerned that a job off-campus could become too much of a distraction and detract from his studies.

Chapter 4: Filling Out Your FAFSA

To apply for financial aid or a federal student loan, you must fill out the Free Application for Federal Student Aid (FAFSA). The FAFSA is a standard form that collects information about your family circumstances, income, and assets, to determine how much financial assistance your student needs to pay for college.

Unless you intend to pay for school completely out of your own pocket and have no desire for any kind of assistance, you should fill out the FAFSA every year. Colleges use the information you provide on the FAFSA to determine your eligibility for the nine federal student financial aid programs, the 605 state aid programs, and for most institutional and private grants and scholarships. You should fill out the FAFSA even if you do not expect to receive federal financial aid or take out a student loan, because your student might be eligible for other types of scholarships or financial aid programs. The FAFSA is used to apply for non-need-based federal programs such as Unsubsidized Direct student loans and the TEACH grant. A student who starts school and discovers later on that he or she does not have enough money to complete an academic year can quickly get an Unsubsidized Direct student loan or a Parent PLUS loan if the FAFSA has been filled out. Both the student and parents must fill out the FAFSA unless the student is independent (see below).

The FAFSA can be filled out online at the FAFSA website (www.fafsa.ed.gov) or on a paper form. The online FAFSA walks you through the application process, with instructions, explanations, worksheets, and automatic calculations. If you prefer to submit a paper form, order one by calling 1-800-4-FED-AID or print the PDF form from the Federal Student Aid website (www.studentaid.ed.gov/PDFfafsa). You can also obtain paper forms from high school guidance counselors and school financial aid offices. Follow the instructions carefully and send your FAFSA in by registered mail so that you have a record of the date.

The FAFSA becomes available each year on January 1 for the upcoming academic year. The federal deadline for submitting the

FAFSA is June 30, but state and school deadlines may be different. You can find out about these other deadlines on the FAFSA website. Fill out the FAFSA as early in the year as you can. Though the Pell grant and Direct student loans are available for everyone who qualifies, each school has limited funding for programs like the FSEOG and federal work study. Those funds are distributed to eligible students on a first-come, first-serve basis. Six states (Illinois, Kentucky, North Carolina, South Carolina, Tennessee, and Vermont) award state grants on a first-come, first-served basis until the money runs out. If you do not submit your FAFSA early, you could miss out on financial aid.

The FAFSA asks for information from your previous year's tax return. If you have not done your taxes yet when you fill out your FAFSA, you can use a FAFSA worksheet to estimate your income and go back and correct the FAFSA when you have completed your tax return.

When you fill out the FAFSA for the first time, you may be confused by some of the questions. The answers to most of your questions can be found in the detailed instructions for filling out the FAFSA. If you cannot find the answer there, call 1-800-4FED-AID (1-800-433-3243) or 319-337-5665 or email your question to FederalStudentAidCustomerService@ed.gov. You can find a wealth of information on the Finaid.com and Fastweb.com websites. Do not let uncertainty about a FAFSA question stop you from submitting your FAFSA on time.

Do not pay for the FAFSA.

Websites that charge a fee for filing the Free Application for Federal Student Aid (FAFSA) are in no way associated with or endorsed by the U.S. Department of Education. There is no charge for filling out the FAFSA. The official FAFSA website is **www.fafsa.ed.gov**. You can get free assistance filling out the FAFSA on the FAFSA website, from the financial aid office at the college you are thinking about attending, from the Federal Student Aid Information Center, or from a high school guidance counselor.

The FAFSA web address has .gov in it. If you are asked for your credit card information while filling out the FAFSA online, you are not at the official government site.

Gather Your Information

Before sitting down to fill out your FAFSA, gather the following information:

- Your Social Security number
- Your parents' Social Security numbers if you are a dependent student
- Your driver's license number if you have one
- Your alien registration number (Green card number) if you are not a U.S. citizen
- Federal tax information or tax returns including W-2 information, for you (and your spouse, if you are married), and for your parents if you are a dependent student: IRS 1040, 1040A, 1040EZ, Foreign tax return, or tax return for Puerto Rico, Guam, American Samoa, the U.S. Virgin Islands, the Marshall Islands, the Federal States of Micronesia, or Palau
- Records of your untaxed income, such as child support received, interest income, and veterans noneducation benefits for you, and for your parents if you are a dependent student
- Information on cash; savings and checking account balances; investments, including stocks and bonds and real estate but not including the home in which you live; and business and farm

assets for you, and for your parents if you are a dependent student

A dependent student will also need most of the above information for his or her parent(s).

Note: Keep copies of all these records in a file or a folder on your computer. You might need them later for verification.

Your Federal Student Aid PIN

You and your student will both need a Federal Student Aid PIN to sign the FAFSA electronically. You can obtain a PIN by going to *www.pin.ed.gov*. For questions about the PIN Web site or specific questions about the PIN, call the Federal Student Aid Information Center at 1-800-4-FED-AID (1-800-433-3243) or 319-337-5665. If you are hearing-impaired and have questions, contact the TTY line at 1-800-730-8913.

Your PIN serves as your electronic signature and provides access to your personal records, so you should never give your PIN to anyone, including commercial services that offer to help you complete your FAFSA.

You can use FAFSA on the Web without a PIN. You will have to print out and mail in a signature page to complete your FAFSA submission.

Keep a record of your Federal Student Aid PIN in a safe place. You will use it to renew your FAFSA each year, make changes and corrections to your FAFSA, sign documents electronically, and access student loan information on the National Student Loan Data System (*www.nslds.ed.gov*).

Student and Family Income

Use income records for the tax year prior to the academic year for which you are applying: for instance, if you are filling out the 2014-15 FAFSA, you will need 2013 tax information.

If you have not done your taxes yet, you can estimate the amounts based on last year's tax return. If your income has changed significantly in the past year, use the "Income Estimator" on the FAFSA income information page to estimate your AGI. After you file your taxes, you will need to log back in to the FAFSA and enter the correct information.

If you have already done your taxes, you might be able to use the online IRS Data Retrieval Tool (IRS DRT) to automatically enter information from your tax return. The tool should be available two weeks after you file if you owed no taxes or paid in full and filed your taxes electronically, and eight weeks after you file on paper. If you filed electronically and still owe taxes, the IRS DRT cannot be used until mid-May, and if you filed a paper tax return with taxes still owing, the information will not be processed until mid-June.

IRS DRT

The IRS DRT takes you to the IRS website, where you log in by providing your name and other information exactly as you provided it on your tax return. You can preview your information before agreeing to transfer it to your FAFSA.

When you return to the FAFSA, questions that are populated with tax information will be marked with "Transferred from the IRS." Do not make any changes to those answers (except where Individual Retirement Account or pension rollovers are involved). Making changes will invalidate the information you retrieved. If you use the IRS DRT and do not change any of the retrieved information in your FAFSA, you will not have to provide tax transcripts if you are selected for verification.

Assets

Some of the FAFSA questions ask about your assets. Assets include checking and savings account balances, brokerage accounts, cash, stocks, bonds, mutual funds, money market accounts, certificates of deposit, trusts, tax credits, college savings plans (529 plans, prepaid tuition plans, Coverdell education savings accounts), real estate (house, land, farm) other than your residence, businesses with over

100 full-time employees, pension plans, life insurance policies and income-producing property.

The EFC calculation factors in 20 percent of assets owned by a student, and a much smaller percent of the parents' assets. Certain assets, such as the net worth of the home you live in, the family car, and qualified retirement plan accounts (pensions, 401(k) plans, IRAs, etc.) are not reported on the FAFSA. The value of small businesses owned and operated by the family is also excluded.

NOTE: Fill out the assets section of the FAFSA, even if you are not required to.
Parents who have an AGI under $50,000 and are eligible to file a simplified federal income tax return, such as an IRS Form 1040A or 1040EZ, qualify for a simplified needs test that disregards all assets. Parents who qualify for a simple needs test do not have to provide asset information. Complete the asset information section of the FAFSA even if you qualify for the simple needs test, because some states and schools use this information for computing their own financial aid awards.

Depending on the parents' age, a certain portion of their assets is excluded from the EFC calculation because the parents are not expected to spend all their retirement savings on a child's education. For parents in their late 40s, this asset protection allowance is around $50,000. Amounts over that are assessed on a sliding scale. Families at the top end of the scale are expected to contribute no more than 5.64 percent of their assets to their children's' education. Less than 4 percent of dependent students have their financial aid eligibility lowered because of parental assets.

You are supposed to enter the assets you own on the day you fill out the FAFSA. For this reason it is a good idea to keep copies of your bank and brokerage account statements in case your FAFSA is selected for verification.

Schools

Each school participating in federal financial aid programs has a Department of Education code number. The online FAFSA allows you to select your schools by name and address from a dropdown list. Each school you select will receive your FAFSA information electronically.

You should list your first choice college first, second choice second, and so on. You can list up to 10 schools on the online FAFSA or up to four schools on a paper FAFSA. If you decide later on to apply to a different school, log in to your FAFSA and add the school to your list. If you already have 10 schools listed, you will have to delete one of them to make room for a new school. The deleted school will no longer receive your financial information electronically.

For each school, you are asked whether you plan to live in on-campus housing or off campus. This is because each school has a different cost of attendance (COA) for each type of living arrangement. The COA is used in calculating your expected family contribution (EFC). If you decide on a different living arrangement later on, notify the financial aid office at your school because you might qualify for a larger amount of federal and state student loans and financial aid.

Schools outside the US that participate in the US federal student loan program also have FAFSA code numbers.

In the section that asks about your interest in different types of financial aid, including work study and student loans, answer each question with "yes." Answering "yes" does not obligate you to accept a loan or work study position, but it leaves these options open for you.

Family Information

Unless you are an independent student, you must include information about your parents on your FAFSA. Your parents will also need to fill out and sign a FAFSA.

For a student filling out the FAFSA:

- If the parents are living and married to each other, answer the questions about both of them.
- If the parents are living together and are not married but meet the criteria in their state for a common-law marriage, answer the questions about both of them. If their state does not consider them to be married, fill out the parent information as if they are divorced.
- If the parent is widowed or single, answer the questions about that parent.
- If a divorced or widowed parent is remarried, or a single parent is married, as of the day the FAFSA is signed, answer the questions about that parent and the stepparent. The stepparent does not have to pay anything for the student's education, but his or her financial information is included in the calculation of the EFC
- When a student's parents are divorced or separated, or biological parents never married, the parent with whom the student lived the most during the past 12 months should fill out the FAFSA. If the student lived the same amount of time with each divorced parent, give answers about the parent who provided more financial support during the past 12 months or during the most recent 12 months that the student actually received support from a parent.

The following people are not considered parents unless they have legally adopted the student: grandparents, foster parents, legal guardians, older brothers or sisters, and uncles or aunts.

An adopted student should follow the instructions above for parents, based on the adoptive parents' current marital status.

On the question about the parents' education level, your parents are considered to be your birth parents or adoptive parents. A stepparent is not the student's parent in these questions.

You may be able to submit your FAFSA without parent information despite being considered a dependent student if you are unable to provide parent information due to the following special circumstances:

- Your parents are incarcerated.
- You have left home due to an abusive family environment.
- You do not know where your parents are and are unable to contact them (and you have not been adopted).
- You are older than 21 but not yet 24, are unaccompanied, and are either homeless or self-supporting and at risk of being homeless.

FAFSA on the Web will ask you whether you are able to provide information about your parents. If you are not, you will have the option to indicate that you have special circumstances that make you unable to get your parents' information. FAFSA on the Web then allows you to submit your application without entering data about your parents.

Although your FAFSA will be submitted, it will not be fully processed without information about your parents. You will not receive an expected family contribution (EFC) and must immediately contact the financial aid office at the college or career school you plan to attend. The financial aid staff may ask for additional information to determine whether you can be considered independent and have an EFC calculated without parent data. Gather as much written evidence of your situation as you can. The financial aid office's decision about your dependency status is final and cannot be appealed to the U.S. Department of Education.

Parents unwilling to provide their information on your FAFSA

When FAFSA on the Web asks you whether you are able to provide information about your parents, say no. On the next screen, select the option that says you do not have a special circumstance, but you still cannot provide parent information.

The FAFSA explains that if your parents do not support you and refuse to provide their information on the FAFSA, you may submit your FAFSA without their information. However, you will not be able to get any federal student aid, and the financial aid office of the school you plan to attend will decide whether you can get an unsubsidized Direct loan. If you agree to this, you may submit your FAFSA without parent information. Your FAFSA information will be sent to the colleges you list, but you won't get an EFC.

You must immediately contact your school's financial aid office to discuss the possibility of getting an unsubsidized loan. The financial aid office may ask for a written statement from your parents, indicating that they refuse to provide their information on the FAFSA and that they no longer support you financially. (Forms of support include allowing you to live in their home, including you on their car or health insurance, providing a car to drive on a regular basis, and payment of your tuition or fees.)

The financial aid office will look at your situation and decide whether you may receive an unsubsidized loan. That decision is final and cannot be appealed to the U.S. Department of Education.

If your parent or stepparent is unwilling to provide parent information, do everything you can to convince them. Point out that they will not have to pay anything for your education or support you in any way, and that the information is only needed so that you can get financial aid or a federal student loan. If you submit your FAFSA without parent information, you will not receive an EFC. Not only will you miss out on federal financial aid, you will not be considered for any private or institutional aid programs that look at the EFC to determine your eligibility for their funds.

For parents filling out a FAFSA:

An unborn child who will be born before or during the financial aid award year (July 1 through June 30) and will be your legal dependent should be counted as a member of the household.

Expected Family Contribution (EFC)

A standard formula, established by Congress, is used by the U.S. Department of Education to evaluate the financial information reported on the FAFSA and to determine the expected family contribution

(EFC). For a dependent student, the fundamental elements in this standard formula are the student's income and assets, the parents' income and assets, the family's household size, the parents' ages, and the number of family members (excluding parents) attending postsecondary institutions. For independent students, the EFC is based on the student's income and assets, and those of his or her spouse if married.

The EFC is the sum of:

- a percentage of net income (income remaining after subtracting allowances for basic living expenses and taxes)
- a percentage of net assets (assets remaining after subtracting an asset protection allowance)

Different assessment rates and allowances are used for dependent students, independent students without dependents, and independent students with dependents.

If more than one child in your family is attending a postsecondary school, the EFC for each child is the family EFC divided by the number of students in the family. The FAFSA does not include parents who are attending college the same year as their child. If a parent is also attending college, ask the financial aid office at your child's school for a professional judgment review. For parents who are enrolled at least half-time in a degree or certificate program at a college eligible for federal student aid, the financial aid officer will either increase the number of students in college to include the parent, or subtract the actual amounts paid for the parent's college education from income. This will result in a reduction in the child's EFC.

Your EFC is not necessarily how much you will pay for a year in college. It is a measure of the family's ability to pay based on income and assets. Schools use the EFC to award need-based financial aid and to determine how much you can borrow in federal and state student loans.

The actual amount you pay out of pocket for a year of school could be much lower or higher than your EFC, depending on how accurately the school calculates its COA, and whether you can find ways to economize. You could spend more if your student chooses a more expensive housing option, joins a sorority or fraternity, travels a lot, participates in clubs and extracurricular activities, or takes courses that require extra supplies and equipment, such as art or architecture. You could spend much less if your student is awarded a merit-based, sports, or academic scholarship, regardless of financial need.

Though the EFC calculation excludes the value of your home from your assets and a living allowance from your income, it is not always an accurate measure of a family's ability to pay for college. For example, it does not consider a family's debt load. The FAFSA does not account for medical bills, car payments, or credit card debt that could consume a family's income during the year. The FAFSA does not count the value of your family residence as an asset, but it does count the money in your bank accounts on the day you fill out your FAFSA. If you have just sold your house or car and that money is in the bank, it is counted as an asset even though you intend to use it to buy a new house or car next week.

Your EFC is on the Student Aid Report (SAR) you receive after you fill out the FAFSA. If your EFC seems too high, or you have a temporary financial situation, like the one above, that makes your income and assets appear greater than they really are, inform your school's financial aid office right away. The financial aid officer might be able to help you make corrections to your FAFSA, or adjust your financial aid award because of exceptional circumstances.

About 250 colleges use an institutional methodology (IM) to calculate a different EFC for their own financial aid awards. The IM EFC includes different types of assets (such as boats and RVs), assumes a minimum student contribution, allows for regional differences in cost of living, gives different allowances for educational savings and emergency funds, treats children of divorced parents differently, and adjusts for more than one child in college at the same time.

Student Aid Report (SAR)

One day after the FAFSA is processed, the student's Student Aid Report (SAR), with information about eligibility for federal financial aid and a list of the student's answers to the FAFSA questions, will become available online.

If the student gave a valid email address on the FAFSA, he or she will receive an email with a link to his or her SAR online. Students who filed a paper FAFSA and did not give an email address will receive a paper SAR in the mail at the address given on the FAFSA. Students who filed an electronic FAFSA and did not provide an e-mail address will receive a paper SAR Acknowledgement in the mail listing their FAFSA information, and asking them to make any corrections at the FAFSA website (www.fafsa.gov). You can log in to the FAFSA website with your PIN to view your SAR.

If you fill out an electronic FAFSA and sign with a PIN, you will receive an e-mail link to your SAR within three to five days or a SAR Acknowledgement in the mail within seven to ten days. If you submit a paper FAFSA and did not give an email address, you can expect to receive your SAR in the mail within two to three weeks.

If your FAFSA is complete, your EFC will appear in the upper right-hand corner of the SAR. If your FAFSA is incomplete there will be no EFC and your SAR will contain instructions telling you what to do next.

Under the EFC on your SAR or SAR Acknowledgement is a four-digit data release number (DRN), which you will need if you choose to allow your college or career school to change certain information on your FAFSA.

Review the information on your SAR and your answers to all the FAFSA questions. If there is a mistake on your SAR, you will need to correct or update your FAFSA on the FAFSA website. If you received a paper SAR, you can correct it by writing in the corrections or updates on the paper SAR, signing it, and mailing it to the address provided on the SAR.

The schools listed in your FAFSA will receive your financial aid information electronically in an Institutional Student Information Record (ISIR) one day after the FAFSA is processed.

Correcting or Updating Your FAFSA

If you estimated your AGI and want to update your FAFSA with information from your completed tax return, need to correct the information on your FAFSA, or want your financial information sent to additional schools, log in to the FAFSA website and select "Make FAFSA Corrections." You will need your Federal Student Aid PIN. Make the changes to your FAFSA and submit your new information.

Many of the items on the FAFSA cannot be changed, because they were supposed to be accurate on the day you filled out the FAFSA. For example, if you had a large amount of cash and have now spent it on a new family car, you cannot alter the amount of cash you reported on the FAFSA. If a significant change in your financial circumstances has occurred, such as the sudden loss of a parent's job, talk to a financial aid officer at your school about making adjustments to your FAFSA. Your contact information, such as your address and email, can be corrected.

If your Social Security number is wrong, you cannot correct it on the FAFSA. Ask a financial aid officer at your school what you should do.

You must report any changes in your dependency status (legal adoption, pregnant with a child who will be born during the award year) except for changes in your marital status.

If you are selected for verification, you must update your FAFSA with any changes in the number of people in the student's household or the parents' household, or in the number of people in the household attending college. If these changes have occurred because the student got married, talk to the school's financial aid officer.

Verification

Sometime after your child has received a financial aid award letter, you might get a letter from your child's school financial aid office asking you to send in copies of your tax return and other documents to support the financial information on your FAFSA. This is no cause for alarm; schools are required to verify information for at least 30 percent of their federal financial aid recipients, and some schools verify 100 percent. There are several reasons why you might be selected for verification:

- You were selected randomly.
- Your FAFSA is incomplete.
- Your FAFSA contains inconsistent data.
- Your FAFSA contains estimated information.
- You elected not to use the automatic IRS Data Retrieval Process. (Applicants who use the IRS DRT are less likely to be selected for verification because their information was drawn directly from their tax returns.)

If you receive notice that you are selected for verification, review your SAR for messages from the U.S. Department of Education. If you have been selected, an asterisk appears after your EFC number on your SAR. Follow the instructions in the SAR or in the letter from the school.

Gather the requested documents and make sure they have all been signed correctly. The school might also ask you to complete a verification worksheet. **Return the documents and verification worksheet to the school as soon as possible. Procrastination might delay the disbursement of your student's loan or financial aid.**

FAFSA verification ensures that the information students and parents report is accurate, and prevents ineligible students from receiving aid by reporting false information.

Dependent and Independent Student

The federal government holds the parents of a college student responsible for paying for higher education until the student is 24 years old. Until the age of 24, a student is considered a dependent student. Federal and state governments will not step in with financial assistance, such as a Pell grant, FSEOG, or Subsidized Direct student loan, unless the student's family has demonstrated financial need by submitting FAFSAs for both the student and the parents. Though Unsubsidized Direct student loans are available to every student regardless of family income, a dependent student cannot receive one unless his or her parents have filled out a FAFSA.

Independent students qualify for higher federal financial aid and student loan limits because they are not receiving money for education from their families. Only an independent student can receive federal financial aid without submitting parents' financial information to the U.S. Department of Education.

A dependent student for financial aid purposes is not the same as a dependent on a federal income tax return. Regardless of whether a parent claims the student as a dependent on a tax return, the student is considered a dependent student unless he or she is:

- at least 24 years old by December 31st of the financial aid award year
- currently an orphan or ward of the court, or was a ward of the court until the age of 18
- a veteran of the Armed Forces of the United States
- a graduate or professional student
- married
- responsible for legal dependents other than a spouse (providing more than half the individual's support)

Most students under the age of 24 are considered dependent students, even if they are supporting themselves financially.

Situations sometimes arise in which a divorced or estranged parent refuses to fill out the FAFSA, leaving the dependent student without access to financial aid or government student loans. Financial aid administrators can override a student's dependency status in special circumstances, but rarely do so unless the student can provide legal documentation of a parent's hostility or neglect, such as court documents, medical records, police records, and reports from social workers or school counselors. The school is answerable to the federal government for every override decision, so financial aid administrators are unable to make the determination without supporting documentation. A parent's refusal to pay for higher education is not considered an exceptional circumstance.

These are special circumstances in which a student under 24 might be declared an independent student:

- The student can provide legal documentation that he or she was sexually or
physically abused by the parents.
- The student's parents are incarcerated or presumed dead.
- The student's parents cannot be located - for example, when a student immigrated
alone to the U.S. and became a naturalized citizen, and has not been able to contact his or her parents.
- The student has been legally adopted by a current guardian who is not a parent.
- The student has been officially determined to be an unaccompanied youth who is
homeless or self-supporting and at risk of becoming homeless.

The student must also provide evidence that he or she is making enough income to support himself or herself financially and is living independently. The financial aid officer will ask to see pay stubs, rent and utility receipts, and other proof that the student is financially independent. A student who is still living at home, or who left home very recently, will be suspect. Rent receipts from a parent are not acceptable.

NOTE: National Association for the Education of Homeless Children and Youth (NAEHY)
More than 58,000 college students declared themselves homeless on the 2013 FAFSA. The National Association for the Education of Homeless Children and Youth (NAEHY) (www.naehcy.org) offers information and resources to help homeless students and school financial aid officers.

To qualify as an independent student because of marriage, a student must have been married at the time he or she filled out the FAFSA. A student who gets a divorce during the year reverts to dependent status the next academic year. In states that recognize common-law marriage, a student may be able to be declared independent if the couple can meet the state criteria for common-law marriage and show that they are financially self-supporting. Young couples will have difficulty meeting all the criteria for a common-law marriage.

A pregnancy could make a student independent, if the baby will be born during the financial aid award year and the mother will provide more than half of the baby's support.

On the FAFSA, a child who is supported by your parents or someone else is not your legal dependent.

EFC Strategies

Do not give false information on your FAFSA to try and lower your EFC. One third of all FAFSAs are verified, and some schools verify all their students' FAFSAs. If the school detects signs of fraud, it is required to notify the Inspector General at the US Department of Education. The Department of Education also uses automated software to find inconsistencies in FAFSAs. You will be required to return all federal financial aid that you received as a result of reporting false information on your FAFSA, and some schools expel students who commit fraud. The penalty for purposely providing false or misleading information on the FAFSA is a fine of up to $20,000 and/or up to 5 years in prison (Section 490(a) of the Higher Education Act of 1965 [20 USC 1097(a)]). You can be penalized just for using false information to apply for student financial aid, whether you actually receive the aid or not.

While you must not enter false information on your FAFSA, there are some things you can do to lower your EFC and maximize your student's eligibility for financial aid. These strategies are not practical for everyone, but you should be aware of how certain financial circumstances could impact your EFC. With some advance planning, you can schedule financial transactions so that they do not increase your EFC.

A student from a higher-income family is not likely to be awarded financial aid, such as the Pell grant, FSEOG, or Subsidized Direct student loans. He or she can qualify for Unsubsidized Direct student loans equal to the school's cost of attendance (COA) minus scholarships and the family's EFC. A lower EFC means the student can qualify for more money in Unsubsidized Direct student loans, and possibly for work study funds.

The annual maximum in federal loans that a student can borrow ranges from $5,500 the freshman year to $7,500 for the junior and senior years, with an aggregate undergraduate limit of $31,000. Independent undergraduate students, whose parents' income is not counted, can borrow up to $4,000 more per year, and professional or graduate students can borrow up to $20,500 per year. If the school has a high COA, even a student with a high EFC might be able to borrow the full amount. A student living at home and receiving a partial scholarship at a local university might be able to borrow only a few hundred dollars in federal student loans.

Your Base Year

When you fill out your first FAFSA during the early spring of your student's senior year in high school, you will be using the tax returns from the previous year - the year your child ended the junior academic year and began his or her senior year. This is your "base year."

The income and asset information on the FAFSA, including your AGI, will come from your tax return for that year, and your child's financial aid awards for the first year in college will be based on the income or assets for that year. Unless your family size increases, your income changes significantly, or additional children start college during the following four or five years, you can expect a similar EFC each year.

If you are planning a large financial transaction such as one-time sale of stocks and securities, sale of a business, or a cash sale or purchase of a house, try to schedule it before the start of your base year or wait until your student's senior year in college, so that the capital gains do not increase your income.

Student Income

A student from a lower-income family, who could qualify for financial aid and Subsidized Direct loans, might jeopardize some of that financial aid by earning too much from a job.

In calculating the EFC, student income is weighted more heavily than family income. However, a certain amount of the student's income, called an income protection allowance, is not counted towards the EFC. For the 2013-2014 academic year, the income protection allowance was $6,130. As long as a student did not make more than $6,130 from employment or a summer job, none of the student's income is counted. Half of any income (minus Social Security tax and income tax) over the income protection allowance is added to the EFC. Every year the US Department of Education issues an *EFC Calculation Guide* with that year's income protection allowance. A student can keep the EFC lower by not earning more than the income protection allowance for that year.

Income from federal work study is excluded from student income in calculating the EFC.

Withdrawals from 529 education savings plans or prepaid tuition plans are not considered income.

Student Assets and Parent Assets

The EFC includes 20 percent of the value of assets in the student's name, such as cash, savings accounts, bonds, mutual funds, stocks, CDs, T-bills, and money market funds. Cash or property given to the student are also counted as student assets.

Some parents' assets are not counted in the FAFSA at all. These include the home the parents live in, family vehicles, retirement savings plans (IRAs, 401(k)s, and pensions) , and businesses with less than 100 employees that are owned and operated by the parents. In addition, depending on the parents' ages, an asset protection allowance shelters a certain amount of the parents' assets. For parents in their late 40s, around $40,000 in assets is excluded from the EFC calculation.

The EFC includes 12 percent of the value of assets above the asset protection allowance. Students do not get an asset protection allowance.

Since student assets are weighted much more heavily than parents' assets, it makes sense to move assets from the student's name to the parents. A student cannot just give assets away to a relative. Custodial accounts and trust funds belong to the student and cannot be transferred to the parents. However, some 529 plans allow the transfer of funds from Uniform Gifts to Minors Act (UGMA) and Uniform Transfer to Minors Act (UTMA) accounts into an education savings account owned by the student. Tax-advantaged education savings accounts such as Coverdell savings accounts, 529 college savings plans and the refund value of 529 prepaid tuition plans are considered part of the parents' assets even if they are owned by a dependent student. Accounts owned by independent students must be reported as student assets.

Series I and EE savings bonds originally purchased by the parents can be transferred into their names, along with noncustodial certificates of deposit and savings accounts opened by the parents in the child's name.

Grandparents or relatives who want to help pay for a student's education should wait until the student's last year in college, or pay off student loans after the student graduates. Money given to the student or spent on his or her behalf is counted as the student's untaxed income on the next year's FAFSA and will result in a higher EFC. Alternatively, the money could be given to the parents, whose assets are shielded and weigh less heavily in the EFC calculation. Also, grandparents and relatives can help by paying for some of the student's personal expenses such as air tickets, clothing, a computer, and dorm room furnishings.

Your financial aid eligibility is calculated based on your assets on hand the day you fill out the FAFSA. You can reduce the amount of cash in both the parents' and student's bank accounts by moving it to assets that are not counted in the FAFSA. For example, if you have been saving money for a big purchase such as a new family car, buy the car before you fill out the FAFSA.

Family consumer debt is not considered in financial aid calculations, so you can lower the amount of your cash assets by paying down your credit card debt, car loan, or mortgage.

The same applies to money that your student has been saving. Before filling out the FAFSA, the student should pay down debts. A student who plans to rent a house or apartment might be able to put down a deposit and the first month's rent. Encourage your student to buy some of the items he or she will need for college, such as bedding and a microwave, early. (A computer is an exception. You might find a better price for a new computer later on, just before school starts, or by using student discounts from your school. Students typically get special low prices for software programs like Microsoft Office and Photoshop.)

A family that is almost destitute will automatically qualify for financial aid and subsidized loans, while a high-income family will not be eligible for these benefits at all. If your AGI is hovering around $50,000, however, you could increase your student's eligibility for financial aid and subsidized loans by taking steps to reduce your taxable income. For example, you could contribute several thousand dollars to an IRA, or delay receiving a bonus until the next tax year.

Be aware of how your financial decisions this year may affect next year's eligibility for financial aid and student loans. Since more weight is given to the student's assets than the parents' assets in calculating the EFC, spend the student's college savings first and the parents' in later years.

Some long-term family plans can also affect eligibility for financial aid. The EFC calculation considers the number of people in the household, and the number of dependent students in college. If a relative is planning to move in with your family, make that move before you start filling out the FAFSA. The EFC is divided by the number of people in the family attending college more than half-time. Parents attending college must request a professional judgment by a financial aid officer in order to be counted.

Bridging the Gap

When you look closely at your financial aid award letter, you might find that the amount of your EFC plus the financial aid and loan package still falls several hundred (sometimes one or two thousand) dollars short of the school's COA. This is called "gapping" – the school has not been able to come up with enough financial support to cover the entire cost of attending the school for a year. The actual gap may be even wider if the school has underestimated the costs of room, board, textbooks, and personal expenses. This gap means that your student will probably run out of cash before the end of each semester. Do not let this become an unpleasant surprise for both of you. Be aware of this possibility and prepare ahead of time. Here are some ways to bridge the gap:

- Take out a private student loan for the amount of the difference between your student's financial aid award and the school's COA.
- Open a revolving credit account such as a dedicated credit card or a home equity line of credit to use for emergency funds. Remember that the interest on a home equity loan can be deducted as mortgage interest on your tax return.
- Help your student make a budget and see if there are ways to save money on the expenses under his or her control, such as rent, travel, food, and textbooks.
- Encourage your student to get a part-time job during the summer and save some money for college expenses.
- Look for a paid internship or part-time job on or near campus to earn extra money during the school year.
- Participate in an AmeriCorps or SCA internship during the summer and earn an education credit. In 2013, the education credit for a 12-week internship was $1,175.
- Apply for scholarships, awards, and special grants related to your student's field of study. You can learn about these through the school and from professional and academic association websites.

Chapter 5: Private Student Loans

Private student loans are available from banks, credit unions, and other financial institutions. Approximately $150 billion of the more than $1 trillion student loan market is private student loans.

Many families take out private student loans to cover the education expenses that are not paid with state and federal loans and financial aid. A family might use a private student loan to pay part of its EFC, or to cover the extra thousands of dollars it costs to go to a private college or pay out-of-state tuition at a state university. Some families borrow private student loans without realizing that lower-interest federal and state loans are available.

Government loan limits have not kept up with the rapidly increasing cost of tuition and room and board at colleges and universities. According to the National Center for Education Statistics, a branch of the U.S. Department of Education, in the 2011-12 academic year, the average in-state tuition increased by 6 percent at community colleges, and by 5 percent at in-state four-year colleges and universities. Tuition increased by an average of 4 percent at private four-year colleges.

Statistics show that the amount borrowed in private student loans always drops when government loan limits are raised. According to the College Board's *Trends in Student Aid 2009*, private student loan volume dropped 50 percent after the *Ensuring Continued Access to Student Loans Act of 2008* increased the annual and aggregate loan limits on the federal Stafford loan starting July 1, 2008.

NOTE: Do not be fooled by private student loan advertising. Aggressive advertising causes confusion about private student loans. Type the words "student loan" in an internet browser, and you are bombarded with a series of paid ads for private student loans and loan brokers, some of which look very official and masquerade as government agencies. Remember that you apply for federal and state loans through your school by filling out the FAFSA.

Private student loans are essentially personal loans tailored for students and their families. They offer some of the same features and repayment options as federal student loans and are similarly protected from being discharged in bankruptcy.

Like federal and state student loans, the amount of a private student loan typically does not exceed the school's COA minus the amount you receive from scholarships, financial aid, and other loans. The lender will verify that you have been accepted for admission at the school before disbursing the loan. You can use the private student loan to pay your EFC, but if you need additional funding, you might have to resort to a personal loan of another type.

Accept all available financial aid and federal and state loans before resorting to a private loan. Private student loans differ from federal and state loans in several important ways:

- Students and parents do not automatically qualify for private student loans. A private loan company will reject your application if you have a low credit score or adverse credit history.
- Interest rates are based on your credit score, and can be as high as 14 percent. You can qualify for a lower interest rate if you have a credit-worthy cosigner.
- You might pay additional fees and commissions.
- Repayment terms might be less favorable. The grace period might be shorter, or you might have to start repaying the loan as soon as it is disbursed. You might be charged a fee when you request forbearance. Options such as income-based repayment might not be available.
- Private loans do not qualify for federal student loan forgiveness programs for health care workers, teachers, or community service internships.
- Private loans cannot be consolidated with your federal loans in a Direct consolidation loan. After you graduate, you will make separate payments for your federal loans and private loans.
- Federal loans are forgiven if the borrower dies before the loan is paid off. Depending on the lender's policies, a borrower's

heirs might become responsible for repaying a private student loan if the student dies.

Shopping for a Private Student Loan

Private student loans are available from banks, credit unions, and other financial institutions. Sallie Mae. Wells Fargo, and Discover are the largest private student loan lenders in the U.S.

Many schools partner with a specific lender and offer customized private loan packages. Applications are processed by the financial aid office and the loans are disbursed through the school. You are not required to use a school's preferred lender for private loans, but the application process might be more streamlined. Compare the terms of the school's private loans with the terms offered by other lenders. Most schools partner with the lenders that offer the best terms for their students, but they might select a lender because it provides convenient online administration or is located in the same state as the school.

If you choose a private lender that is not affiliated with your school, the certification process might take a little longer and delay disbursement of the loan. This delay should not be more than a few days, even if you have to mail in a paper certification form. If you have not heard from the school or lender after a week, contact them to see if there is a problem with the application.

When shopping for a private student loan, examine all aspects of the loan carefully. When you sign the loan documents, you are entering into a legal contract and you will be bound by its provisions. These are some of the factors to consider:

- **Interest rate.** What is the interest rate? Is it fixed or variable? If variable, is there a maximum and minimum limit to the interest rate? Is the maximum interest rate reasonable? The low advertised interest rate is probably available only to borrowers with a very good credit score. What will your interest rate actually be?
- **Estimated monthly payment and estimated total cost.** When the loan enters repayment, what will the monthly payment be?

How much will you repay, including interest and fees, if you follow the standard repayment schedule?

- **Deferment and forbearance.** What deferment options does the loan offer? Is there a fee for forbearance? If the interest accrues during forbearance or deferment, how much more will the monthly payment be?
- **Fees.** Is there a loan origination, insurance, or disbursement fee? Is the fee added to the principal when the loan enters repayment, or is it subtracted from the loan amount when the loan is disbursed? If it is subtracted when the loan is disbursed, you will not receive the full amount or money that you borrowed.
- **Requirements.** What documents are you required to provide? Can you qualify for this loan?
- **Grace period.** Is there a grace period? When does loan repayment begin?
- **Repayment incentives.** Does the lender offer any repayment incentives, such as an 0.25 interest rate deduction for automatic debit, or an interest rate deduction for making a certain amount of monthly payments on time?
- **Loan consolidation.** Does the lender offer private student loan consolidation for this loan?
- **Borrowing limits.** How much can you borrow? Will you be able to borrow enough to cover your education expenses?
- **Repayment options.** Is there a graduated repayment option, in which the first monthly payments are lower and the payment amount increases later when the borrower's career becomes established. Does the lender offer any options if the borrower is unable to make regular monthly payments because of unemployment or underemployment? What are the penalties if the loan goes into default?
- **Cosigner release.** Some private student loans allow the cosigner to be removed from the loan after a certain number of on-time payments. A few loans, including Sallie Mae's Smart Option loan release the co-signer from repaying the loan if the student borrower dies or becomes permanently disabled.

When you are comparing private student loans, do not compare only the interest rates. Look at fees and repayment incentives. Fees can offset the financial benefit of a low interest rate. A 4 percent fee is approximately equal to adding another 1 percent to the interest rate. A loan that offers repayment incentives could cost less in the long run than a loan with a lower interest rate.

A number of websites offer student loan comparisons or search for the best interest rates. If you use these sites, remember that some of them base their calculations on the lowest advertised interest rate. Depending on your credit rating, your interest could be higher. Only about 20 percent of borrowers qualify for the lowest advertised rates. Once you have narrowed your selection down to a few lenders, find out exactly what your interest rate will be and the overall cost of the loan for each lender. You cannot learn what your interest rate will be until you submit a loan application and the lender reviews your credit history.

> **NOTE: Use loan analyzer software to compare private student loans.**
> Finaid.org compares private student loans and provides a Loan Analyzer Calculator to help you compare loan programs (www.finaid.org/loans/privatestudentloans.phtml).

Cosigners - A Family Affair

Interest rates for private student loans are based on the borrower's credit score and the market rate. A student with a low credit score could end up with an interest rate as high as 14 percent, which translates into tens of thousands of dollars over the life of a loan. To get the best interest rate, the student needs a cosigner with a good credit rating. Though you can help your student get a lower interest rate by cosigning the loan, remember that by becoming a cosigner you take on serious financial liability.

You should not cosign a student loan unless you have a genuine commitment to helping that person get an education. If your student is not able to make the loan payments at any time after graduation, you become responsible. If the loan goes into default, your credit rating will be undermined, and you could have difficulty getting a mortgage or a car loan even though you have always been a conscientious borrower. Some types of employment require you to maintain good credit, and if you are looking for a new job, the defaulted student loan could disqualify you.

Even a serious and highly qualified graduate may need more than six months to find steady employment with a good salary. Be prepared for the possibility that you will have to help with loan payments after the grace period ends in order to maintain your own credit rating, or that you will have to help out during periods of unemployment.

Some private loans offer the option of releasing the cosigner from financial liability after a certain number of loan payments have been made on time. The student borrower must be able to demonstrate the ability to pay off the loan.

Unlike other types of personal debt, student loans cannot be easily discharged in bankruptcy.

Federal and state loans have standard interest rates, repayment options, and cancellation policies. The terms of private loans vary from lender to lender. Before signing the loan agreement, study the promissory note carefully and make sure you understand all the terms. Shop around to see if better loan options are available, even if the private loan is offered through the school's financial aid office. When you are talking to your bank or credit union, find a sales representative who understands student loans well.

Before cosigning a loan, ask yourself these questions:

How well do you know your student?
Is he or she likely to complete the degree or program of study, and find a job afterwards? Can you trust him or her to keep up with financial responsibilities and plan for the monthly loan payments? If not, you will be doing both of yourselves a favor by declining to cosign the loan.

Is the degree worth the price?
Will this particular course of study lead to a job that will provide enough compensation to pay off the loan? Private loans do not have the same income-based repayment options as federal and state loans.

Has the student exhausted all avenues for financial aid and government loans?
If the student is not receiving the maximum amount of government loans, your family might have exceptional circumstances that could increase eligibility if you request a professional judgment from a financial aid officer at the school.

Is there some other way to fund this portion of the education expenses?
Do you have an asset that could be sold, or could the student find part-time employment? The goal is to borrow as little as possible.

NOTE: A cosigner's death can put a private student loan into default.
Some private student loans become immediately payable in full if the cosigner dies. If this happens, a student borrower who has been making on-time payments might suddenly find that the loan has gone into default. Before committing to a loan with a cosigner, find out what the lender will do if the cosigner dies before the loan is paid off.

Private student loans and bankruptcy

In 2005, Congress changed the status of private student loans in bankruptcy to match the status of federal student loans. A private student loan cannot be discharged in bankruptcy unless you can demonstrate that repaying the loan would cause you and your family extreme hardship. Consumer advocates argue that because private student loans charge high interest rates based on your credit score, require a cosigner, and set their own loan limits, they should not receive special protection under bankruptcy laws.

Sallie Mae

The Student Loan Marketing Association (Sallie Mae) was created in 1972 as a Government-Sponsored Enterprise (GSE) to support the Federal Family Education Loans (FFEL) program created by the *Higher Education Act of 1965*. At that time, schools and government administrators determined loan amounts, and then students entered into loan agreements with private lenders who supplied the funds. The lenders financed the loans with private capital, and the federal government subsidized fees and interest rates and insured the lenders against default.

Sallie Mae used money from the U.S. Treasury to buy federally-guaranteed student loans from banks, so that the banks could have available cash to initiate new student loans. During the 1980s, Sallie Mae began borrowing its funds from financial markets and no longer relied on the U.S. Treasury. Between 1997 and 2004, Sallie Mae became a private company. In 2005, Sallie Mae represented 45 percent of all federally guaranteed student loans. It also expanded into loan servicing, debt collection, and the private loan business.

A Congressional Budget Office review in July 2009 showed that this system was wasteful and inefficient, and estimated that the government could save $80 billion over ten years by doing the lending itself. After the passage of the *Health Care and Education Reconciliation Act of 2010*, the federally guaranteed loans issued through Sallie Mae were replaced by the Federal Direct Loan program. Under the Direct Loan program, the federal government lends to students directly at fixed interest rates, using federal funds supplied by the U.S. Treasury. Sallie Mae continues to be one of the primary loan servicers for federal student loans, as well as collecting on defaulted debt. Sallie Mae is also one of the largest three private student loan providers in the U.S.

If you borrowed a student loan after 2010 from Sallie Mae, it was a private loan. However, the U.S. Department of Education assigns Sallie Mae as the loan servicer for some new federal student loans.

The Sallie Mae Smart Option Student Loan® offers both fixed and variable interest rates, repayment incentives, and no origination fee. It is the only private student loan offering graduated repayment. If the student opts to begin paying interest, or to make monthly payments, while still in school, the interest rate is 1 percent lower

Chapter 6: Making the Most of Your College Dollars

After your home, your child's college education is one of the largest purchases you will ever make. The 2014 price tag for a year at a private college could be as high as $60,000 per year. What you actually spend will depend on where your student goes to school, whether the student lives at home, how many years he or she takes to graduate, and whether he or she receives scholarships and financial aid.

Treat a college education like any other important purchase. Make sure your money is well spent. Shop around, compare, and find the deal that gives you the best value for your dollars, not only when you are applying for student loans, but when your student is selecting a school and choosing classes and living options. Once you have committed to a school, do everything you can to protect your investment.

What Could Go Wrong?

Getting your student into college and financing that first year is only the first step. Most freshmen start school expecting to graduate in four years with a college degree. However, the data gathered every year from all schools who participate in federal student loan and financial aid programs shows that only about 52.3 percent of college students graduate within 6 years from the university where they enrolled as freshmen. This statistic does not tell the whole story, because approximately one third of students transfer to another school and do not get counted in the graduation numbers for the school where they originally enrolled. Another recent study found that only 31.3 percent of students at public universities, and 52.4 percent of students at private, nonprofit, institutions, graduate in the traditional 4 years. There is a real possibility that you will be borrowing to pay for five or six years of college instead of four, or that your student could be one of those who leave school without earning a college degree, but with student loan debt to pay off.

There are numerous reasons why students stay in school longer than expected, or drop out without finishing:

Immaturity.
A young person who is immature might fail some classes because he or she cannot manage time well and concentrate on studies when surrounded by so many social distractions. For many students, college is the first experience of living away from home, and being together day and night with so many others of the same age is overwhelming. College students are expected to be responsible for attending classes and completing assignments without supervision, and some do not know how to cope with this new freedom. An inexperienced student may not be able to recognize when he or she is in trouble, or be unwilling to seek tutoring or counseling.

Changing majors.
The student may decide to pursue a different major that requires additional classes. According to the National Center for Education Statistics (NCES), about 80 percent of students in the U.S. end up changing their major at least once during their college careers. High school does not expose students to many of the specialties that are taught in college. Many incoming freshmen receive little or no vocational counseling, and realize after they have taken a few classes that they are in the wrong field. Older students may realize that they want to pursue a different career. Some of the classes required to complete a major are not available every semester, and the student may have to stay in school longer to take them.

Illness, stress, or mental instability.
A student may have to withdraw from school because of illness or an injury. Academic pressure and stress sometimes trigger depression or mental instability, so that the student struggles with grades or has to take a break.

Loss of motivation.
A student may simply lose interest in studying, or decide that the classes are not teaching useful skills. After two or three years of making effort to get assignments in on time and study for exams, the student may no longer feel the academic effort is worthwhile.

Unsuitable environment.

The academic or social environment at a particular school may not be suited to the student. A shy, artistic student might be unhappy in a large, sports-oriented university. Some state university campuses are almost empty on weekends because so many of the students go home, while other schools teem with social and cultural activities. A minority student may feel lonely and uncomfortable at a school that lacks cultural diversity. A student who is inadequately prepared for the coursework may become frustrated because classes are too difficult. Some students are unsatisfied when class sizes are large and there is little personal interaction with the professors. A student who does not feel at home at a school is more likely to drop out.

Job or family.

A student who has children to take care of or a demanding job might find that he or she does not have the time to devote to schoolwork. Schoolwork can be pushed down the list of priorities when a student is caught up with the practical responsibilities of a regular work schedule.

Mrs. B:
My daughter continued to work as a waitress at a popular restaurant during her first year at nursing school. At the end of the year, all the nursing students had to take an exam which would determine whether they would be admitted to the next stage of the nursing program. Her test score was just ½ of a percent below the cutoff point, and she was dropped from the program. She is certain that if she had been able to spend more time studying, she would have scored much higher on the exam.

Mrs. J:
While studying for his criminology degree at a local state college, our son took a job as a security guard in a Target store. He found the work interesting. It was much easier to show up for regular shifts at Target than to sit down and do his reading assignments, and he quickly fell behind on his class work. He dropped several classes just before the final exams and had to retake them. He eventually got his degree, but it took two years longer and cost much more than if he had just concentrated on school.

Financial burden. As college costs rise from year to year, the financial burden becomes heavier, and some families and students decide it is not worthwhile to continue. Some students simply cannot find the financial resources to continue paying for college. Others leave school because they feel they must return to their families to help with financial or medical emergencies.

Protecting Your Investment

A college degree is a serious investment. As a parent, you cannot force your student to succeed, but you can be prepared with alternative plans when everything does not go as you expected. Your student is an individual, not a statistic. You know your child's strengths and weaknesses. Be conscious of the unique circumstances that could affect his or her academic career.

There is a delicate balance between wanting to protect your child and not exerting too much control over his or her life. Young people mature through making their own choices and experiencing the consequences. However, a typical 17-year-old about to make a life-altering decision is not equipped with a 40-year-old's wisdom and experience. Help your child to make an informed decision by informing yourself. Communicate with your child about expectations and priorities. You might not agree about everything, but at least you can understand each other's points of view. Stand back, but be ready to step in if you see that your student needs help managing a difficulty. It is your student's life, but your entire family will bear some of the burden if the student fails, drops out, or is unhappy.

Below are some things you can do to protect your investment in education by helping your student succeed while keeping costs under control.

Select a school that is a good fit for your student.

Help with your child's college search, and make sure that your high school student is aware of the available options. Your student is more likely to succeed academically and complete a degree at a school where he or she feels happy and stimulated. Once you have narrowed down your choices, visit each school if possible.

You can use the College Search on The College Board website (https://bigfuture.collegeboard.org/college-search) to find schools that meet specific criteria. The Princeton Review (www.princetonreview.com/rankingsbest.aspx) and the U.S. News and World Report (http://colleges.usnews.rankingsandreviews.com/best-colleges/rankings) release annual profiles of top-ranked colleges. Unigo College Rankings (www.unigo.com/Colleges) ranks schools according to reviews by students.

Visit your state education website to learn about all the schools in your state, then read reviews and rankings to find out what their strengths and weaknesses are. In addition to the large and well-known state universities, many states have smaller colleges and professional schools as well as specialized residential programs on larger campuses.

> **NOTE: The "Student Right-to-Know and Campus Security Act" (P.L. 101-542),** passed by Congress November 9, 1990, requires institutions eligible for Title IV funding to calculate completion or graduation rates of certificate- or degree-seeking, full-time students entering that institution, and to disclose these rates to all students and prospective students.

You can get a better sense of whether a particular school will suit your child from former students. Talk to friends and acquaintances who have attended the schools your child is interested in. An out-of-state school may have a local alumni association in your area. If not, the school's alumni association might be able to put you in contact with a former student who would be willing to talk to you. Ask about their personal experiences and their recommendations for making the most of the opportunities offered at the school.

Pay in-state tuition.

Before you opt for an expensive private college, take a look at your state universities. State schools and universities receive state funding and charge state residents lower tuition than they charge out-of-state students. State universities often have government research contracts and business partnerships that provide local work opportunities for students and valuable job training and experience. Some states offer scholarships, subsidies, and incentives to qualifying students who attend state universities.

Though state schools are notorious for being large, many offer programs that place students in smaller, more specialized community settings. Not all state schools are large universities; community colleges, technical training schools, and specialized academies often come under the umbrella of state universities. Students at newer satellite campuses of a state university might find themselves receiving more personal attention from professors in smaller classes and enjoying more modern dormitories and amenities than students at an expensive private college.

Many states have reciprocal agreements that allow students to pay in-state tuition at state universities in adjoining states or regions. If you are looking at an out-of-state public university, ask if there is a tuition discount for students from your state or students studying a particular major. State universities also participate in study-abroad programs and reciprocal arrangements that allow students to study for one or more semesters in another school.

NOTE: Out-of-state tuition at some state universities is still a bargain.

At some state universities, out-of-state tuition is only a few hundred dollars more than in-state tuition, and other costs such as dormitory housing might be lower than at state universities in your state. Some state universities offer highly-ranked academic programs that are equivalent to the programs of prestigious private schools. It might be worth paying a few hundred dollars more per semester for a quality education at a public university in another state.

Take some general education classes at a local university or community college and transfer the credits.

Many universities accept credits for general education classes taken at affiliated schools. These classes can be taken during a summer break, or for one or two semesters before your student enters a four-year college. Consider taking lower-level mathematics, chemistry, biology, social science, and language classes at a less expensive school, and more specialized classes from the highly qualified professors at a more prestigious university. Before you enroll in these classes, verify that the credits will be accepted to fulfill your university's educational requirements. Many students save money by getting a two-year associate's degree at a community college and then complete a four-year degree at a major university.

Choose a major or a field of interest early.

Universities offer hundreds of majors, and encourage students to try a variety of classes until they "find their passions." However, a student who changes majors too many times may discover that he or she needs to spend an extra year in school to complete all the educational requirements for a major. Some classes are only offered once a year, and some cannot be taken without first completing a series of prerequisite studies. Once a student has decided on a field of study, he or she can participate in related organizations and clubs, volunteer for events, and apply for internships that will enhance the learning experience and establish a network of friends and professors in the same field. Encourage your student to work with an academic advisor and create a study plan that will complete the major within four years. A good academic advisor will steer your student through all the requirements in a reasonable amount of time.

Switching majors too many times can also impact a student's eligibility for financial aid. The Pell Grant is restricted to 12 semesters of study and does not cover classes taken during summer semesters. Students receiving federal student loans are given 150 percent of the number of the semesters or credit hours required for their primary degree program. A student who switches to a major with a shorter time frame or needs extra semesters to complete required classes may not be eligible to receive federal grants or loans during those final semesters.

> **NOTE: A parent's influence can delay changing a major.**
> Many students testify that, though they realized after a few classes that they wanted to switch to another field of study, they delayed changing their majors because they knew their parents wanted them to pursue a particular career. By the time they finally made the switch, they were so far along that they had to stay in school an extra year or more to complete their degrees. Be sensitive to your child's talents and interests, and careful about projecting your own desires and dreams onto your child.

Build a resume.

Four years pass quickly, and then your student is out in the world, looking for a job or trying to get into a graduate program. Encourage your student to take advantage of the many opportunities available on a college campus to gain practical experience, interact with academics and professionals, and build a network of friends and acquaintances. Clubs and organizations give your student a chance to learn new skills and gain leadership experience. Participation in community service projects, campus publications, organized events, jobs on campus, academic research, internships, and study abroad programs adds to your son's or daughter's resume and shows initiative. The experiences gained through these activities may be as valuable as the academic knowledge taught in classes.

When a student begins applying for professional jobs or graduate study programs, he or she will be asked to provide references from professors and employers. Personal relationships with professors and mentors can lead to job opportunities and positive recommendations.

Be practical when choosing living arrangements.

Weigh the costs and advantages of every option. Many universities encourage freshmen students to live on campus in a dormitory with a mandatory food plan for the first year until they become accustomed to student life. Even if it is not mandatory, it is a good idea to purchase a food plan for a student living in a dormitory so that he or she does not have to worry about shopping and cooking while studying and attending classes. A student who does not have a car may find it difficult to get to and from a good grocery store every week.

A student cannot prepare regular healthy meals in a dorm room with a microwave and small refrigerator. Though some dormitories have communal kitchens, most students are not going to cart cooking supplies back and forth to the kitchen every day to prepare their meals. Students living in apartment-style dormitories with two or three roommates sharing a kitchen are more likely to succeed at shopping for and cooking their own meals. You know your child; select an arrangement that will ensure he or she eats well without overspending.

University food plans are typically outsourced to private companies and the meals cost almost the same as modest restaurant meals. Calculate the cost per meal for each food plan, and choose the option that best suits your child's lifestyle. Is your child really going to show up three times a day, seven days a week, for a full breakfast, lunch and dinner? Most students get the best value from a food plan that allows them one or two full meals per day and some flexible spending options at campus eateries. Some students do not use campus food services during the weekends because they return home or are involved in activities away from campus. The food service at a small school may not offer enough variety and your student may soon grow tired of the food. Do not pay for services that your student is not likely to use.

> **NOTE: Check out the food options during student orientation**
>
> At the first university new-student orientation I attended, the food service proudly displayed a hamburger, French fries, and a large milkshake near the entrance, with a sign proclaiming that students would be able to eat meals like this every day. While this display might appeal to a hungry teenager, do you really want your child on a steady diet of French fries and sodas?
>
> Food services typically offer healthy choices such as wraps, salad bars, and fresh fruit, but these can also become tiresome if the quality is not good. Check food service schedules for weekend hours; you may find that cafeterias close early on Saturdays and Sundays, leaving few options for an evening meal. On the other hand, an unlimited food plan may allow your student to stop by and pick up a cookie or a snack between meals, which avoids spending money in coffee bars and fast food restaurants.

The cheapest living situation is not necessarily the best. Consider your child's personality and study habits when deciding on housing options. A cramped dormitory room shared with two other people may be the least expensive option, but is not the ideal study environment. For a first-year student, however, dormitory living provides an opportunity to meet friends of a similar age and level of maturity. Often the friends made during a student's freshman year in the dormitory remain part of his or her social circle for the next four years. Universities typically assign a resident advisor (RA) for each floor of a dormitory to monitor the students, help them get to know each other, and provide advice and support. Dormitories try to protect students by enforcing security procedures and controlling who enters the buildings.

A student who has already established friendships and social contacts will not feel isolated living in an off-campus apartment. In some university towns, sharing a house or apartment with one or two other students is cheaper than living in a dormitory room, while in other towns off-campus housing is scarce and expensive. Some campuses are surrounded by privately owned student apartment complexes with amenities like gyms, pools, and computer labs. When weighing your options, remember to allow for the cost of utilities, internet, and furniture, all of which are typically included in the price of a dormitory room. Also consider transportation to class and the security and safety of your student, who may be returning from the library or social activities late at night.

Buy or rent textbooks online.

You can buy used textbooks or rent textbooks from numerous online booksellers for much less than you would pay for textbooks at the campus bookstore. Many professors now post their book lists online early to give students a chance to buy books online before classes start.

There are times when it makes sense to buy books from the campus bookstore. A recently published book will cost about the same online because you have to buy it new and pay for shipping. (Depending on the subject matter, an older version of a textbook could be just as useful - many professors will tell the students if the latest edition is really necessary, or tell them which parts of the book have been changed.)

If you need your student loan money to buy textbooks, the financial aid office will usually arrange a certain amount of advance credit at the campus bookstore so that you do not have to wait for your loan to be disbursed to get your books. This is especially helpful for freshmen, who might not receive their first loan disbursements until 30 days after classes start.

As soon as the semester is over, sell the textbooks you do not need any more online. Do not wait too long because they could become outdated. Other students will want to buy your textbooks at the beginning of the next semester.

Monitor your child's academic progress and mental health.

A student who is financing an education with student loans and federal grants can suffer serious financial consequences if he or she does not do well in school or drops out. The student is legally obligated to repay student loans whether or not he or she completes a degree program. A student who takes out several semesters' worth of student loans and then drops out of school will find himself or herself responsible for the debt, without the qualifications to get a higher-paying job.

A student receiving need-based (Title IV) financial aid, including the Pell Grant and Subsidized Direct student loans, must attend class for 60 percent of a semester to earn a full semester of financial aid. When a student withdraws from class before the end of a semester, the financial aid office will calculate what percentage, if any, of the financial aid must be returned to the federal government. Part of the money that was disbursed directly to the student may have to be returned.

Dropping one or two classes because of a heavy workload could reduce a student's status to less than full-time. The amount received from a Pell Grant will be recalculated as a lower amount and the student will be responsible to pay back the difference. Student loans go into repayment six months after a student becomes less than half-time. Deferment will be reinstated if the student returns to full-time status the following semester, but interest will have accrued on any Subsidized Direct student loans.

Poor grades or withdrawing from or dropping too many classes will lower the student's completion rate (see *Chapter 3*). If academic performance does not improve after one semester, the student will lose eligibility for federal financial aid, and may not be able to finance the completion of his or her degree.

Most schools raise tuition for required classes that have to be re-taken more than once because of failing grades. Not only will the student be paying for the same class twice or three times, but the cost will go up each time.

Schools encourage students' independence. At family orientations, parents are urged to stand back, let their children make their own decisions, and avoid calling or contacting their children too often. Parents cannot see their child's grades online unless the student gives permission. You know your child well. It is important to foster independence, and you should not attempt to interfere with personal decisions concerning your child's future career. At the same time, you need to protect the financial investment you and your child are making in a college education. Question your student about his or her major. Confirm that your student is working with an academic advisor, and that he or she is taking the required courses.

Be alert for signs that your child is struggling in school, and guide him or her to take steps to remedy the situation before it turns into a crisis. For example, a student can talk to a professor about arranging for tutoring, a financial aid advisor to determine whether dropping a class will affect financial aid, or a mental health counselor for help with personal problems.

Many first-year students are mature enough to take full responsibility and, with some guidance from their academic advisors and the financial aid office, manage their finances, their class schedules, and their academic careers. Others are broadsided by the sudden freedom they encounter in their new environment, confused by the hundreds of choices they are expected to make, or overwhelmed by the academic demands of college classes. According to a study by U.S. News and World Report, one in four freshmen drop out during their first year, and in some schools the freshman dropout rate is as high as one in three students.

Unlike high school teachers, who hand out and oversee homework assignments on a daily or weekly basis, college professors are likely to hand out a schedule of assignments and a reading list on the first day of class or post it on the campus intranet. It is up to the student to read this information and keep up with the class schedule. If you know your child is likely to struggle with time management and study habits, look for a school that has a good program of counseling and mentorship for incoming students. This is reflected in the school's freshman retention rate – the percentage of freshmen who return to the school as sophomores.

A new social environment is not an automatic cure for social awkwardness, low self-esteem, lack of self confidence, and loneliness. Even the most confident high school graduate may face challenges when placed in an unfamiliar or highly competitive social milieu. At the same time that a student is learning to manage new-found academic freedom, he or she must navigate a confusion of personalities, emotions, new friends, and social rules. There may be times when a student feels overwhelmed or unable to cope.

No one can perform well when he or she is ill, suffering from depression or anxiety, or grieving over a romantic breakup or the loss of a loved one. An academic schedule demands regular class attendance and long hours of concentration. A semester goes by quickly, and a student can fall behind in just two or three weeks. A student who is not able to keep up with class work because of personal difficulties may be able to make other arrangements with professors to complete coursework. Before withdrawing from any classes, the student should consult a financial aid advisor about the possible effect on financial aid eligibility, and find out whether any financial aid or loan money will have to be returned.

Be especially vigilant if your student has had problems with drugs or alcohol during his or her high school years. These problems can recur and intensify in a college environment and will eventually result in academic difficulties. Question your child about his or her activities and friends, visit from time to time, and watch for signs of trouble. If substance abuse is sabotaging your child's academic career, do not hesitate to intervene. Both you and your child will bear the financial and personal consequences if you do not.

Compassionate or Medical Withdrawal

A student who is forced to drop out of classes after the drop-add period because of serious illness (including mental illness), or because of the death or serious illness of a family member, may be able to obtain a compassionate or medical withdrawal.

Most schools have a compassionate or medical withdrawal policy that will refund tuition and part of the room and board costs (if the student is living in a campus facility) for a student who withdraws from classes under these special circumstances. The student or the student's family must provide documentation to support the request, including a letter explaining the reason for the withdrawal, doctors' letters, and a suggested plan for the student's future return to school. Ask the school about its specific requirements and any official forms that must be submitted.

If your student is taking medication for a mental health condition, or is under treatment for depression or a mental illness, maintain regular contact with his or her doctor and keep up with appointments and check-ups. This will make it easier to obtain the necessary documentation and prevent your being financially penalized in case he or she becomes ill and needs to take some time off from school.

NOTE: Students keep secrets from their parents.
One of my daughter's friends became mentally unstable, stopped going to class, and spent the next semester at school doing nothing, without ever telling his parents. He managed to get a medical withdrawal through a school counselor and a local psychiatrist, and his parents were not informed because he was not a minor. Another daughter had a roommate with personality problems who became addicted to MySpace. She spent hours every day on the internet and had to be constantly reminded when class assignments were due. Her first semester, she forgot to go to the final exam for her history class because her boyfriend had spent the night. She eventually graduated after seven years, but had to take some classes three times. Her parents never knew what was impeding her success.

Shop for health insurance.

Your student will have medical expenses during his or her college years. Young and healthy students participate in activities that can lead to injury, such as bicycling, hiking, sports, skiing, and martial arts. They also live in close proximity to hundreds of other young people and compromise their immune systems by eating poorly and missing out on sleep. Unexpected medical bills could sabotage all your financial planning. You do not want fear of spending money to keep your child from seeing a doctor when he or she is sick or in pain.

Before your student starts school, evaluate his or her medical needs and investigate all your insurance options to find the one that offers the protection you want at the best price. Under the current law, young people are covered until the age of 26 by their parents' health insurance from an employer. Your monthly premium for family coverage through your employer is likely to be lower than the monthly premium for an individual student health insurance plan. Compare the benefits offered by each plan, and make sure your insurance plan covers health care providers in the city where your student is going to school. If the health care providers in that area are out-of-network, compare the co-pays and deductibles you pay under each plan.

Some schools automatically enroll students in the college's health plan and include the fee on each student's bill. A college health plan might offer full medical services, or it might only offer access to a walk-in clinic on campus. At some schools, students can receive free or inexpensive treatment on campus for simple injuries, infections, colds, and flu. Most campuses make some form of mental health counseling available to all students. A school that makes health insurance mandatory for all its students might waive the health services fee if you prove that your child has other health insurance.

Schools that do not have a college health plan often partner with a health insurance company that sells student insurance packages. The monthly premium for a student health plan can be as much as $200 a month. Before committing to the school health insurance plan, shop around and compare the plans offered by other health insurance companies.

If your student is already receiving subsidized medical insurance through a state or federal program, this coverage will continue until the student reaches the cut-off age. An independent student might qualify for Medicaid or for a subsidized state health insurance plan, based on low income. In some states, family planning clinics offer inexpensive services for women.

A student who works part-time at a company that offers health insurance for its employees might qualify for that plan if he or she works a certain number of hours each week.

> **NOTE: Ask your student to consult you before going to the emergency room!**
> Students who are on their own for the first time are often worried or frightened when they become sick, and may decide to rush to the emergency room without realizing the financial consequences. My friend was landed with an $800 bill when her daughter went to the emergency room and got antibiotics for an ear infection. Make an agreement that your student will call you before going to the emergency room.

Communicate with the school's financial aid office.

At the beginning of a semester, your student might feel too busy to wait in line at the financial aid office, or might be reluctant to discuss financial matters with a stranger. Coach your student to handle his or her own affairs and to get answers promptly to any questions about loans or financial aid. If student loan money is late showing up in your student's bank account, he or she might have missed signing a document or given the wrong bank information. The sooner problems like this are resolved, the sooner your student can get on with school.

Timing is important. At most schools, the drop/add period before a student's class schedule is finalized is only two or three days, and the withdrawal or course drop period during which a student can have tuition refunded after withdrawing from a class is seven to ten days. A student who drops to less than half-time enrollment, or withdraws from too many classes, could lose eligibility for financial aid or subsidized student loans and might be required to return some of the money.

It is better to know exactly what your student's financial situation is from the beginning, so that you can anticipate whether you will need to find extra money to get through the semester. Your student might need to look for a part-time job, or you might need to take out a Parent PLUS loan to make up the shortfall. Your student will experience less stress and anxiety if he or she clearly understands what to expect. Over a college career, your student will also need to consult the financial aid office when changing majors, or if he or she needs to stay on extra semesters to take required classes for a major. The time restrictions on federal student loans could leave your student in a financial bind.

Your Financial Aid Advisor

The information you report on your FAFSA is used by the school to determine your student's eligibility for federal financial aid, the Pell grant, federal subsidized student loans, and scholarships and loans available through the school. Your options are presented in an award letter, and you can accept or decline each one. In many cases the process goes smoothly and you can take care of everything online, including signing your master promissory note. If you have difficulty understanding your award letter, or believe that there has been an error in your FAFSA, call or visit the school financial aid office.

The employees in the financial aid office can help your student navigate the student loan process and offer many kinds of support, including help with budgeting and emergency loans. There is no particular degree or course of study for becoming a financial aid officer. Each school has its own educational requirements and training process for its financial aid staff. Many financial aid officers began their careers as students working in a financial aid office and worked their way up. Financial aid officers receive continuing education through professional organizations such as the National Association of Student Aid Administrators (www.nasfaa.org) and the federal government.

The staff working at the front desk of the financial aid office can look up your records, answer questions about your student loans and financial aid awards, and check whether your documents have been signed and your loans have been disbursed. If your family or student has complicated financial or personal circumstances, or you think a mistake has been made, make an appointment to see the financial aid director or a more senior financial aid officer. A financial aid officer has the authority to determine whether a student under the age of 24 can be declared independent in order to receive more financial aid, and when a student's eligibility can be restored after a period of academic probation or a suspension due to a drug-related conviction. You should also see a financial aid officer if you were unable to adequately explain your personal circumstances when filling out your FAFSA.

Federal financial aid and subsidized student loans are benefits based on family income, and the rules governing them are as stringent as the US tax code. Before making a determination, a financial aid officer may ask you some very personal questions, and request documentation such as court documents, doctors' letters, financial statements, and marriage or death certificates. Prepare for your interview by gathering all the available evidence to back up your story. Do not be offended by personal questions, and try to work together with the financial aid officer to find a solution for your difficulty.

Even though a financial aid officer is very sympathetic, if you do not meet the requirements to qualify for certain benefits, he or she might not be able to help you. Do not blame the financial aid officer for your disappointment. The financial aid officer is responsible for making sure that rules are followed and federal and state money is used in the way it was intended. He or she did not make the rules.

Chapter 7: Paying Off Student Loans

A student has six months (nine months for Perkins loans) from the day of graduation or leaving school (the separation date) before he or she must begin paying off student loans. This is known as the grace period, and it goes by very quickly.

In an ideal world, your student quickly finds a lucrative job, preferably before the end of the six months, and is able to pay off the student loans early and begin saving for retirement. In reality, it often takes longer than six months to find a good job, particularly in today's fickle job market. Many recent graduates have to navigate through a series of internships and low-paid entry level positions before they establish themselves in a career. Loan obligations cannot be ignored, but several repayment options, as well as deferment and forbearance, help a borrower manage during difficult times. It is important to know how much you are expected to pay to whom and when, and to keep in contact with your student loan servicer. When you are not able to make your monthly loan payments, talk to your student loan servicer about your situation. Do not let your student loans go into default.

Gathering Your Information

Depending on where your student goes to school and how much you borrow, you are likely to have more than one type of student loan by the time you graduate, each with its own interest rate, loan servicer, and repayment terms. You could have federal and state student loans, Parent PLUS loans, and possibly private loans. Soon after your student leaves school, gather all your loan information in one place. You can find out which types of federal student loans you borrowed by looking up your account on the National Student Loan Data System (NSLDS) website (www.nslds.ed.gov). You will need your U.S. Department of Education PIN to access your student loan account. Each loan is listed separately. Information on your private student loans is not available on this website.

Your school is your loan servicer for Perkins loans. If you borrowed Perkins loans, state loans, or private loans through your school financial aid office, you will receive instructions for repaying those loans and statements from the school's loan servicers. If you borrowed private student loans from an outside lender, you are responsible for setting up payment arrangements with that lender.

The interest rates on student loans can vary from year to year. Each loan has the interest rate for the academic year in which it was first disbursed. Some loans have fixed interest rates and some have variable rates that fluctuate from time to time. On the National Student Loan Data System website you can find a list of all your federal loans and the interest rate for each one. If you have several federal student loans with different interest rates, it is possible to refinance them with a federal consolidation loan with a fixed interest rate.

Fixed Rate Loans			
Borrower	Type of Loan	Date of First Disbursement	Fixed Interest Rate
Undergraduate Students	Direct Subsidized and Unsubsidized Loans	7/1/13 - 6/30/14	3.86%
		7/1/06 - 6/30/13	6.80%
	Direct Unsubsidized Loans	7/1/11 - 6/30/13	3.40%
	Direct Subsidized Loans	7/1/10 - 6/30/11	4.50%
		7/1/09 - 6/30/10	5.60%
		7/1/08 - 6/30/09	6.00%
		7/1/06 - 6/30/08	6.80%
Graduate and Professional Students	Direct Unsubsidized Loans	7/1/13 - 6/30/14	5.41%
		7/1/06 - 6/30/13	6.80%
	Direct Subsidized Loans	7/1/06 - 6/30/12	6.80%
Parents and Graduate and Professional Students	Direct PLUS Loans	7/1/13 - 6/30/14	6.41%
		7/1/06 - 6/30/13	7.90%

If you borrowed federal student loans before 2011, you could have Federal Family Education Loans (FFEL) or Stafford Direct loans, each of which has its own interest rates and repayment terms. The FFEL program was established by the *Higher Education Act of 1965* and discontinued on June 30, 2010, by the *Health Care and Education Reconciliation Act of 2010.* Between 1965 and 2010, more than 60 million Americans paid for education expenses with FFEL loans. The FFEL program was replaced by the Federal Direct student loan program in 2010. Under the Direct student loan program, the federal government lends to students directly at fixed interest rates, using federal funds supplied by the U.S. Treasury.

The tables below show the interest rates for various federal loans disbursed since the 2006 - 2007 academic year. You can find detailed information about interest rates for various loan types on the Federal Student Aid website (www.direct.ed.gov/calc.html).

Variable Rate Loans			
Loan Type	Date of First Disbursement	Loan Status	Interest Rates for the Period 7/1/12 to 6/30/13
Direct Subsidized and Unsubsidized Loans	7/1/98 to 6/30/06	Repayment/Forbearance	2.39%
		In-School/Grace/Deferment	1.79%
Direct PLUS Loans	7/1/98 to 6/30/06	Any Status	3.19%

  Gather the statements from each of your loan servicers and make a record of their contact information and the dates the first payments are due. If you have several loans with the same loan servicer, the loan payments are typically combined into one monthly payment.

Your Student Loan Servicer

A loan servicer is a company that handles the billing and other services for your federal student loan. The loan servicer sets up repayment plans and loan consolidations, processes payments, maintains loan statements, and files your annual IRS Form 1098-E.

The U.S. Department of Education (ED) assigns your loan to a loan servicer after the first disbursement is either transferred to your school account, deposited in your bank account, or both. (Student loans are typically disbursed in two payments, once at the beginning of each semester.) Soon after that you will receive a welcome letter and loan information from your loan servicer. The loan servicer will continue to send you regular interest statements, and when your student's grace period is ending, you will receive a notice that the first payment is due. It is important to maintain contact with your loan servicer, and to update your contact information whenever your mailing address, telephone number, or email address changes.

If you have several loans with the same loan servicer, you will generally make one monthly payment to cover all of them. You can find out who is the loan servicer for your federal student loans on the NSLDS website.

The four primary federal student loan servicers are:
   SLM Corp., or Sallie Mae
   Nelnet
   FedLoan Servicing, or the Pennsylvania Higher Education
Assistance Agency
   (PHEAA)
   Great Lakes Higher Education Corporation & Affiliates

The Not-For Profit (NFP) federal loan servicers are:
   Aspire Resources Inc.
   CornerStone
   COSTEP
   EDGEucation Loans
   EdManage
   ESA/Edfinancial
   Granite State – GSMR
   KSA Servicing
   MOHELA
   OSLA
   VSAC Federal Loans

Your loan servicer is your contact when you want to request deferment or forbearance, change your payment plan, or are having difficulty making your monthly payments. Simple transactions, such as making payments and updating your contact information, can be done through your loan servicer's website or by phone. If you have a more complicated situation, such as a wrong payment or a request for deferment during military service, you need to speak to a customer service representative. Unfortunately, you cannot just walk into your loan servicer's local neighborhood office. Contact has to be by telephone or email, and it can be difficult to reach someone who has the knowledge authority to assist you.

NOTE: Student loan servicers are evaluated four times a year.
The Department of Education (ED) assigns loans to loan servicers based on a scoring system. Four times a year, ED releases a *Servicer Performance Report* that ranks loan servicers in five categories: defaults by number of loans, default by dollar amount, and surveys of borrowers, schools, and federal loan personnel. ED awards new loan volumes to loan servicers based on their scores in these categories.

Consumer advocates all point out the lack of consumer choice as one of the factors contributing to the loan servicers' poor customer service record. You cannot shop around for the best loan servicer; you are stuck with the one assigned to your loans by the U.S. Department of Education (ED). You might be able to move your loans to another servicer through a loan consolidation.

The Consumer Financial Protection Bureau (CFPB), established in 2010 to investigate possible abuses by the financial services industry, has launched an investigation into the customer service practices of student loan servicers. In addition to difficulty accessing customer service representatives, the CFPB is looking into allegations that instead of helping borrowers with financial difficulties to set up income-based repayment plans, Sallie Mae channeled them into forbearance, which will cost them more money in the long run. Before contacting a customer service representative at your student loan servicer, study the options on the loan servicer's website so that you understand the offers being made to you.

From time to time, the U.S. Department of Education may move your loans from one servicer to another. If this happens, you will receive a welcome letter and contact information from your new loan servicer.

MM: Sallie Mae customer service nightmare

Sallie Mae's customer service representatives can answer simple questions over the phone. If your request is more complicated, you need a lot of patience. Count on spending an hour or more on the phone. The regular customer service representatives are not trained to resolve those types of issues. It seems as though their goal is to be so vague that you will eventually just give up and go away. If you persevere long enough, you can eventually get through to a higher-level supervisor and learn what you need to do.

On one occasion, a representative told me I could not get a private loan deferment for Peace Corps service, but that there was a deferment for AmeriCorps. Based on that information, I declined the Peace Corps and took an internship with the Student Conservation Association (SCA), only to learn from a more knowledgeable customer service representative that private loans never qualify for deferment. I could have gone into the Peace Corps - the financial consequences would have been the same.

When I called to apply for an extended repayment plan to lower my monthly payments, the first representative I spoke to did not know what I was talking about, and another tried to get me to pay a fee and sign up for forbearance. Finally I reached someone who was able to tell me where to fax the necessary application documents.

MM: Sallie Mae customer service nightmare (cont'd):
On another occasion, I paid off a high-interest private loan three or four business days before the scheduled automatic debit was due. The loan pay-off was not posted quickly enough, and the scheduled monthly payment was deducted from my bank account. After spending hours on the phone and faxing bank statements and a letter requesting a refund, I was informed that Sallie Mae simply did not have a means of reversing the automatic debit. I never did get my $370 back – it went into limbo somewhere.

When you are late with a student loan payment, you will start receiving computer-generated telephone messages from cheerful people with cheerful names like "Hayley" and "Kristin" asking you to call an 800 number. Write this phone number down and use it to contact your loan servicer. From my experience, the customer service representatives at this number have more knowledge and more authority to set up payment plans and help resolve other issues.

Exit Counseling

When a student with student loans graduates, leaves school, or drops below half-time enrollment, he or she is required to undergo exit counseling. This may take place in person with a financial aid advisor, or online. Follow your school financial aid office's instructions for exit counseling. Many schools direct you to the Exit Counseling link on the Federal Student Loan website (*https://studentloans.gov/myDirectLoan/index.action*) where you will be asked to sign in with your Department of Education PIN. Some schools use the exit counseling on the website of Mapping Your Future (*www.mappingyourfuture.org/OSLC*), a non-profit organization sponsored by some of the student loan guaranty agencies.

The school will put a hold on your academic records until it receives official verification that you have completed exit counseling.

A typical exit counseling session lasts about 30 minutes. Like entrance counseling, exit counseling informs the student of his or her rights and responsibilities regarding repayment of the loan. The student is also told about repayment options. Some exit counseling includes advice on finances and budgeting. During exit counseling the student will be asked for a current phone number, email address, phone number, and other contact information.

Repayment Options for Government Loans

A standard student loan repayment schedule consists of a series of 120 payments made over a 10-year period. If you have a fixed interest rate, the repayment schedule consists of the same fixed monthly payment for a specified number of years. You know in advance how much is due every month, and that makes it easier to budget. Monthly payments for loans with variable interest rates will vary as the interest rates fluctuate. As with a mortgage, the first loan payments are applied mostly to the interest, while later payments pay off more and more of the capital. If you enter a period of deferment after having made payments for several months or years, smaller monthly payments will be recalculated based on the remaining balance when you re-enter loan repayment.

The standard monthly payment for a $45,000 loan at 6.8 percent interest would be $517.86. There are many reasons why a recent graduate might have difficulty coming up with a $500 payment every month, including a low-wage job in a slow job market, or periods of unemployment or unsteady employment. To help a borrower manage loan payments and stay out of default, several repayment options are available for federal student loans. State government loans have similar options.

Income-based repayment (IBR) plans allow you to pay as little as 10 percent of discretionary income (the difference between your AGI on your tax return and 150 percent of the poverty guideline for your family size and state of residence) as your monthly payment. Because the repayment period is extended to 20 or 25 years, you will pay more interest over the long run, but the smaller monthly payments will be more manageable. A borrower who does not qualify for income-based repayment can use the Graduated or Extended repayment options to lower monthly payments. As long as you qualify, you can change from one plan to another when your circumstances change. The important thing is to keep your loans current, and to keep in contact with your student loan servicer(s).

Standard Repayment

A payment is made every month for 10 years. If the loan is a small one, the payment is at least $50 per month until the loan is paid off. This option costs you the least because you pay less in interest. However, the monthly loan payment is higher. The monthly payment is approximately 1.15 percent of the total amount of the loan.

Graduated Repayment

The first monthly payments are lower, but the payment amount is increased every two years, so that the loan is paid off in 10 years. This is a good option if you expect your salary or income to increase regularly over the next few years. The lowest monthly payment is never less than the amount of interest that accrues between payments, and no single payment under this plan will ever be more than three times greater than any other payment. You will pay more in interest under this plan because the capital is paid off more slowly.

Extended Repayment

The monthly payments are smaller and the loan is paid off in 25 years instead of 10 years. The borrower ends up paying more in interest over time. To qualify for extended repayment:

- You must have borrowed for the first time after October 7, 1998.
- You must have more than $30,000 in either FFEL or Direct loans. (Only a FFEL or a Direct loan over $30,000 qualifies. You cannot combine the two types of loans.)

Income Contingent Repayment

Each year, your monthly payments will be calculated on the basis of your AGI (plus your spouse's income if you're married), family size, and the total amount of your Direct loans. Each monthly payment is the lesser of:

- the amount you would pay if you repaid your loan in 12 years, multiplied by an income percentage factor that varies with your annual income, or

- 20 percent of your monthly discretionary income.

If the monthly payments are not large enough to cover the interest that has accumulated on the loans, the unpaid amount will be capitalized (added to the loan capital) once a year. This capitalization will not exceed 10 percent of the original amount you owed when you entered repayment. Once that limit is reached, interest will continue to accrue but will no longer be capitalized.

The maximum repayment period is 25 years. If you have not fully repaid the loans after 25 years, the unpaid portion will be forgiven. The amount that is forgiven will be taxable income in the year the loan is discharged. Time spent in deferment or forbearance does not count as part of the 25 years.

This repayment option is not available for Parent PLUS loans, or for consolidation loans which include amounts from Parent PLUS loans.

Income-Based Repayment (IBR)
The monthly payments are never more than 15 percent of your discretionary income. As your income changes, the amount of your monthly payment changes.

To qualify, you must have a partial financial hardship, meaning that the monthly payment on your IBR-eligible federal student loans under a 10-year Standard Repayment Plan is higher than the monthly payment under IBR.

While you have a partial financial hardship, interest that accrues but is not covered by your loan payments will not be capitalized. This includes interest accrued during a period of deferment or forbearance.

Every year, you must provide documentation of your income and family size to your loan servicer. If you fail to do this, your monthly payment amount will increase to the amount you would be required to pay under the 10-year Standard Repayment Plan, based on the amount you owed when you began repaying under IBR. Unpaid interest will also capitalize.

If your monthly IBR payment amount does not cover the interest that accrues on your loans each month, the government will pay the unpaid accrued interest on Direct Subsidized loans or Subsidized Federal Stafford loans (and on the subsidized portion of Direct or FFEL Consolidation Loans) for up to three consecutive years from the date you begin repaying your loan under IBR.

The maximum repayment period is 25 years. If you have not fully repaid the loans after 25 years, the unpaid portion will be forgiven. The amount that is forgiven will be taxable income in the year the loan is forgiven. Time spent in deferment or forbearance does not count as part of the 25 years.

Your monthly payments under IBR will be smaller, but you will pay more in interest than if you had paid off the loan in 10 years.

If you make 120 on-time, full monthly payments under IBR while you are employed full-time for a public service organization, you may be eligible to receive forgiveness of the remaining balance of your Direct Loans through the Public Service Loan Forgiveness Program.

This repayment option is not available for Parent PLUS loans, or for consolidation loans which include amounts from Parent PLUS loans.

Pay As You Earn
This option is available only to new borrowers: borrowers who had no outstanding balance on a Direct Loan or FFEL Program loan as of October 1, 2007, and received a disbursement of a Direct Loan on or after October 1, 2011.

Only Direct Loans are eligible for the Pay As You Earn repayment plan, though your FFEL Program loans are taken into account when determining whether you have a partial financial hardship. You will need to select another repayment plan, such as the Income-Based Repayment plan, for any FFEL Program loans that you have.

Paying Off Student Loans

To qualify for Pay As You Earn, you must have a partial financial hardship (your monthly payment under the 10-year Standard Repayment Plan would be higher than your monthly payment under Pay As You Earn).

Under Pay As You Earn, your monthly payment amount will be 10 percent of your discretionary income and will never exceed the amount you would be required to pay under the 10-year Standard Repayment Plan.

Your payment amount may increase or decrease each year based on your income and family size. Once you have initially qualified for Pay As You Earn, you may continue to make payments under the plan even if you no longer have a partial financial hardship.

Any loan balance remaining after 20 years of qualifying repayment will be forgiven. The amount that is forgiven will be taxable income in the year the loan is forgiven. Time spent in deferment or forbearance does not count as part of the 20 years.

Every year, you must provide documentation of your income and family size to your loan servicer. If you fail to do this, your monthly payment amount will increase to the amount you would be required to pay under the 10-year Standard Repayment Plan, based on the amount you owed when you began repaying under IBR. Unpaid interest will also capitalize.

If your monthly IBR payment amount does not cover the interest that accrues on your loans each month, the government will pay the unpaid accrued interest on Direct Subsidized loans or Subsidized Federal Stafford loans (and on the subsidized portion of Direct or FFEL Consolidation Loans) for up to three consecutive years from the date you begin repaying your loan under Pay As You Earn.

While you have a partial financial hardship, interest that accrues but is not covered by your loan payments will not be capitalized, even if interest accrues during a period of deferment or forbearance. If you are determined to no longer have a partial financial hardship, unpaid interest capitalizes, but the total amount of interest that capitalizes is limited to 10 percent of your original principal balance when you began paying under Pay As You Earn.

If you make 120 on-time, full monthly payments under Pay As You Earn while you are employed full-time for a public service organization, you may be eligible to receive forgiveness of the remaining balance of your Direct loans through the Public Service Loan Forgiveness Program.

This repayment option is not available for Parent PLUS loans, or for consolidation loans which include amounts from Parent PLUS loans.

Repaying Parent PLUS Loans

The repayment period for a Parent PLUS loan disbursed before July 1, 2008, began 60 days after your school made the last disbursement of the loan. For Parent PLUS Loans first disbursed on or after July 1, 2008, payment can be deferred while the student for whom you obtained the loan is enrolled at least half time, and for an additional six months after the student graduates or drops below half-time enrollment. (half-time enrollment status is determined by your child's school). You must request the deferment period separately for each loan.

Parent PLUS Loan borrowers may only choose from the standard, extended, or graduated repayment options. To be eligible for the extended plan, you must have more than $30,000 in Direct PLUS Loan debt and you must not have an outstanding balance on a Direct Loan as of October 7, 1998. Depending on the repayment plan you choose, you will have from 10 to 25 years to repay the loan.

Your loan servicer will notify you of the date your first payment is due. If you do not choose a repayment plan, your loan servicer will place you on the standard plan, with fixed monthly payments for up to 10 years. Most Parent PLUS borrowers stay with the standard repayment plan, but the other options are available for borrowers with larger loans who need to make lower monthly payments.

If you find yourself unable to make the regular monthly loan payments, contact your loan servicer. You might be able to arrange a different payment plan with lower payments, qualify for a deferment, or apply for a temporary forbearance.

If your monthly payment is not received by the due date, your loan becomes delinquent. If you fail to make a payment, you will receive a reminder that your payment is late. If your account remains delinquent, you will receive warning notices reminding you of the consequences of default and of your obligation to repay your loans. Late fees may be added, and your delinquency will be reported to one or more national credit bureaus.

Parent PLUS loans do not qualify for income-based repayment options.

You can use the calculators on the Federal Student Aid website (*http://studentaid.ed.gov/repay-loans/understand/plans/standard/comparison-calculator*) to anticipate what your monthly payment will be. Be aware of the due date of your first payment and plan for it.

Repaying Graduate PLUS Loans

Repayment on a Graduate PLUS loan is deferred while the student is enrolled in school at least half time. That deferral ends six months after the student's enrollment drops below half time, or the student leaves school.

Interest accrues on the Graduate PLUS loan while the student is in school. This accrued interest can be repaid at the end of the grace period, or capitalized - added to the loan capital.

Graduate and professional students who borrowed PLUS loans are eligible for all the repayment options available to borrowers of Direct student loans, including loan consolidation.

Graduate PLUS loan holders are also eligible for Public Service Loan Forgiveness. If they make regular loan payments for 10 years while working at a nonprofit, in government, or at another qualifying organization, any outstanding debt is forgiven. If the borrower dies or becomes permanently disabled before the loan is completely repaid, the remaining balance will be canceled.

Direct Loan Consolidation

As a result of the annual limits placed on various types of federal and state student loans, and the frequent changes in interest rates and policies, a student borrower may graduate with a variety of loans to be paid off, each with its own interest rate, loan servicer, and repayment terms. A Direct Consolidation loan replaces multiple federal loans with one new loan, a single monthly payment, and in some cases, new repayment terms.

The advantages of a Direct Consolidation loan are:

- It simplifies your monthly payments.
- You can lower your monthly loan payment by extending the new loan repayment period to 30 years.
- Variable interest loans are converted to a fixed interest rate.
- Consolidating your loan might make you eligible for repayment options that were not available before for some of your loans.

The disadvantages are:

- You could lose the borrower benefits from some of your original loans, including interest rate discounts, principal rebates, or some loan cancellation benefits. The original loans disappear when they are paid off by a consolidation loan, and you cannot reverse that process later on.
- You will make more payments, and pay more in interest, when you extend the repayment period to more than 10 years.

The following loans are eligible for consolidation:

- Direct Subsidized Loans
- Direct Unsubsidized Loans
- Subsidized Federal Stafford Loans
- Unsubsidized Federal Stafford Loans
- Direct PLUS Loans

- PLUS loans from the Federal Family Education Loan (FFEL) Program
- Supplemental Loans for Students (SLS)
- Federal Perkins Loans
- Federal Nursing Loans
- Health Education Assistance Loans
- Some existing consolidation loans

Parent PLUS loans cannot be included in a Direct Consolidation Loan. Private loans are not included in the Direct Consolidation Loan program. Some private lenders offer consolidation loans of their own.

A Direct Consolidation Loan has a fixed interest rate for the life of the loan. The fixed rate is the weighted average of the interest rates of the loans being consolidated, rounded up to the nearest ⅛ of 1 percent. The interest rate will never exceed 8.25 percent.

To qualify for a Direct Consolidation Loan, you must:

- have at least one Direct Loan or FFEL Program loan that is in a grace period or in repayment
- either make satisfactory repayment arrangements for any defaulted loan with your current loan servicer before you consolidate, or agree to repay your new Direct Consolidation Loan under the Income-Contingent Repayment Plan or the Income-Based Repayment Plan

After the Direct Consolidation Loan has been approved, you have 180 days to add additional loans to the consolidation. After that, you will have to submit a new application. Generally, you cannot consolidate an existing consolidation loan again unless you include an additional Direct loan or FFEL Program loan in the consolidation.

You can apply for a Direct Consolidation loan after you leave school or drop to half-time enrollment. You can apply online at the Direct Consolidation loan website (*www.loanconsolidation.ed.gov*) or call 1-800-557-7392 (TDD/TTY: 1-800-557-7395).

If you consolidate your loans while one of them is in its six-month grace period, you will lose the remainder of the grace period for that loan. Subsidized Direct loans that are consolidated with Unsubsidized Direct loans will lose the subsidized interest benefit if your consolidated loan enters deferment while you return to school or serve in the Peace Corps.

Before submitting your application for a Direct Consolidation loan, consider all your repayment options carefully. The Direct Consolidation loan website has a calculator that will show you your new interest rate and the amount of the new monthly payment. You will need your Department of Education PIN to use the calculator.

Ask yourself these questions:

- Do I need to simplify my monthly loan payment process?
- How much lower will my monthly payment be?
- How much longer will it take to pay off my loans, and how much more will I pay in interest over the repayment period?
- Do any of my loans have special loan cancellation benefits, such as health care
service loan cancellation? If you have already put in some years towards Public Service Loan Forgiveness for one of your loans, you will lose those years when that loan is consolidated. The entire new loan may be eligible for Public Service Loan Forgiveness, but you will have to start counting the years over again.

If your main concern is lowering your monthly payments to get through a temporary financial difficulty, you might be able to use forbearance or deferment instead of loan consolidation.

NOTE: Watch out for private loan consolidation scams.
Private loan companies frequently run aggressive internet ads offering student consolidation loans. You might even get phone solicitations. If you consolidate your federal student loans using a private consolidation loan, you will lose all federal repayment benefits, such as in-school deferment, Public Service Loan Forgiveness, and the chance to pay off a portion of your loan with an AmeriCorps or SCA internship. Federal Direct Consolidation loans are only available directly through the Direct Consolidation loan website (*www.loanconsolidation.ed.gov*). All official government websites have .gov in the website address. There is no application fee for a federal consolidation loan. Avoid any website that charges a fee of any kind for a federal consolidation loan. Unless you are consolidating only private student loans, do not fill out an application through any website that does not have .gov in its address.

Perkins Loans

Perkins loans are federal student loans but they are disbursed, administered, and serviced by your school rather than the Department of Education. Questions about repaying your Perkins loan must be directed to the school that issued the loan.

Interest rates, repayment options, and cancellation benefits for Perkins loans are different than for Direct loans. For example, the grace period is nine months rather than six months. Perkins loans have loan discharge programs for military service and loan cancellation for teachers working at schools in low income areas. Interest on Perkins loans is subsidized during periods of deferment. Perkins loans can be consolidated with other federal student loans in order to qualify for Public Service Loan Forgiveness or to simplify your loan payments. Before consolidating a Perkins loan, however, study your options carefully. The Perkins loan has a fixed 5 percent interest rate; your new loan will have a higher interest rate that is calculated by averaging the interest rates on all your loans. When you consolidate a Perkins loan with a Direct consolidation loan, you lose any special loan cancellation benefits, and the payments you have already made on your Perkins loan will not count towards loan forgiveness.

To consolidate a Perkins loan, you have to have at least one other federal student loan, such as a Direct loan or an older FFEL.

Repaying Private Loans

The repayment terms for a private student loan are detailed in the loan contract. Most private student loans offer a six-month grace period and a payment schedule similar to government student loans. However, they do not have the same income-based repayment options as government loans. Private student loans are not eligible for Public Service Loan Forgiveness or for loan cancellation through service in the Peace Corps, AmeriCorps, or the Student Conservation Association (SCA).

Many private student loans are eligible for deferment if the student returns to school. You will have to consult the lender about deferment under other circumstances, such as active military service or service in the Peace Corps. A private lender may charge a fee for putting your loan in forbearance.

Private consolidation loans pay off your existing student loans and replace them with a new loan. You might be able to get a better interest rate if your credit rating has improved since you first borrowed the student loans, and a different repayment plan.

Do not use a private consolidation loan to pay off federal or state student loans because you will lose the additional repayment benefits of those government loans.

If you have difficulty making private student loan payments because of economic hardship, contact your lender to see what kind of repayment options you can negotiate. You may be able to extend your payment schedule and lower your monthly payments with a private consolidation loan, or apply for forbearance.

Repayment Incentives

Repayment incentives are financial rewards for making loan payments on time. Federal student loans offer two types of repayment incentives:

- **Interest Rate Reduction for Automatic Withdrawal Payments**
  You can receive a 0.25 percent interest rate reduction if you arrange for your bank to automatically debit loan payments from your account every month.

- **Up-Front Interest Rebate**
  You may receive an up-front interest rebate on a Direct Subsidized Loan, Direct Unsubsidized Loan or Direct PLUS Loan. The amount of the rebate is equal to a percentage of the loan. It is as if your interest rate had been reduced by that percentage. Your loan statement indicates whether you received an up-front interest rebate.

  The up-front interest rebate is given to you when the loan is disbursed, but to keep it you must make all of your first 12 required monthly payments on time (the loan servicer must receive each payment no later than six days after the due date). If you fail to make 12 monthly payments on time, the loan servicer will add the rebate back to your loan principal, increasing the amount that you have to repay.

An FFEL Program loan might offer similar repayment incentives. Contact your lender for more information.

Repayment incentives for private loans vary from lender to lender, and are one of the factors you should consider when you are shopping for a private loan. Repayment incentives that might be available from a private lender include:

- **Automatic Payment Discount** - an interest rate reduction for setting up automatic payments through a bank account each month
- **Relationship Discount** - interest rate discounts for borrowers who already have a checking or savings account with the bank

- **Cosigner Release** - the option to release a cosigner from any loan obligations after a certain number of on-time payments
- **Graduation Reward** - a principle balance reduction, usually about 1 or 2 percent of your outstanding loan principle, upon graduation. This incentive is intended to encourage borrowers to complete their degrees, because default rates are much higher among those who drop out before finishing school.
- **On-Time Payment Reward** - an interest rate reduction after you make a certain number of on-time payments (12, 24, 36, or 48)

NOTE: Repayment incentives can save you hundreds of dollars.

Do everything in your power to fulfill the conditions for repayment incentives, because you will save hundreds of dollars over the life of your loan. Statistics show that only about 15 percent of borrowers succeed in making on-time payments for the designated time period. The on-time payment reward is not as helpful as it seems if the interest rate reduction is not applied until after you have made three or four years' worth of on-time payments, because by that time your loan principle will have decreased.

Public Service Loan Forgiveness

Public Service Loan Forgiveness (PSLF) is intended to encourage graduates to enter and remain in public service careers. After 120 full, on-time, payments made while a borrower is working in public service, the balance of the loan is forgiven. A full payment is one that equals or exceeds the amount of the scheduled monthly payment. A payment is on-time if it is made within 15 days of the due date. The payments do not have to be consecutive. Each payment must be made individually; you cannot make a lump-sum or one-time payment. (An exception is made for Peace Corps and AmeriCorps volunteers who receive an education award or a stipend after they complete a term of service.)

Any employment with a federal, state, or local government agency, entity, or organization or a not-for-profit organization that has been designated as tax-exempt by the Internal Revenue Service (IRS) under Section 501(c)(3) of the Internal Revenue Code (IRC) qualifies for PSLF. It does not matter what type of work you do for these organizations, or what type of services they provide.

Public service jobs include jobs with federal, state, local or tribal government organizations, public child or family service agencies, 501(c)(3) non-profit organizations, tribal colleges or universities, the military, and public schools and colleges.

Employment with a private not-for-profit employer that is not a tax-exempt organization under Section 501(c)(3) of the IRC may qualify if the organization provides certain specified public services. These include emergency management, military service, public safety, or law enforcement services; public health services; public education or public library services; school library and other school-based services; public interest law services; early childhood education; public service for individuals with disabilities and the elderly. The organization must not be a labor union or a partisan political organization.

Businesses organized for profit, labor unions, partisan political organizations, organizations engaged in religious activities (unless the qualifying activities are unrelated to religious instruction, worship services or any form of proselytizing) do not qualify.

You must be employed full-time by the organization on the dates that you make each of the 120 payments. You are employed full-time if you work at least 30 hours a week for the organization. Time spent in religious instruction or other religious activities does not count as part of the 30 hours. A teacher or contractor is a full-time employee if he or she works eight months of the year and the employer considers that to be full-time employment. If you work for more than one public service organization and the combined hours equal at least 30 hours per week, you are a full-time employee.

To benefit from PSLF, you must repay your loans with the Income-Based Repayment (IBR), Pay As You Earn, or Income-Contingent Repayment (ICR) plans which lower your monthly payments to a percentage of your income. If you use the Standard 10-Year repayment plan, your loan will be paid off in full in 120 payments, and there will be no balance left to forgive. There is a risk; if you do not qualify for PSLF by completing 120 payments while employed in public service, these income-based repayment plans will end up costing you more in interest.

PSLF applies only to Federal Direct loans. FFEL loans and Perkins loans can become eligible if they are consolidated with a Direct Consolidation loan. Only payments on the new Direct Consolidation loan will count toward the required 120 qualifying payments for PSLF. If you made qualifying payments on a Direct loan and then consolidated it into a Direct Consolidation loan, you must make 120 qualifying payments on the Direct Consolidation Loan.

It will take at least 10 years to complete the 120 payments. Keeping track of loan payments and periods qualifying public service employment for such a long time can become complicated. The U.S. Department of Education has created a tracking process and an *Employment Certification for Public Service Loan Forgiveness* form (Employee Certification form), available from the Studentloan.gov website. Part of this form is filled out by your public service employer. Fill out this form annually or whenever you change jobs and submit it to FedLoan Servicing (PHEAA) (www.myfedloan.org/). PHEAA is the PSLF loan servicer. Once PHEAA has verified that your public service employment qualifies for PSLF, all of your federal student loans will be transferred to PHEAA. You might be asked to provide additional documentation to support your employer's eligibility as a public service organization, or to show that you are employed full-time. PHEAA will also evaluate loan payments you have already made to see if they can qualify as part of the 120 payments.

Submit your employer's certification of employment while you are still employed at an organization or soon after leaving it. If you have not already done this, you will be required to submit an Employment Certification form for each employer at the time that you apply for forgiveness.

The first borrowers will be able to claim PSLF in October, 2017. When you have completed the 120 full, on-time payments, you will submit an application for PSLF. You must be working at a qualified public service organization at the time you submit the application and at the time the loan is forgiven. As with other types of loan forgiveness, the amount that is forgiven might taxed as income on your income tax return for that year.

> **NOTE: Older loans must be consolidated to qualify.**
> Public Service Loan Forgiveness is part of the Direct loan program. If you have old FFEL loans from before 2007, you must consolidate them with a Direct Consolidation loan to qualify for loan forgiveness. All federal student loans are eligible if they are included in a Direct Consolidation loan.

Many states offer student loan forgiveness for health care workers or teachers who work in areas of need for a specified period of time. Check with your employer and on your state website to see if you qualify for one of these programs.

Teacher Loan Forgiveness

If you teach full-time for five complete and consecutive academic years in certain elementary and secondary schools and educational service agencies that serve low-income families, and meet other qualifications, you may be eligible for forgiveness of up to a combined total of $17,500 on your Direct Subsidized and Unsubsidized loans and your Subsidized and Unsubsidized FFEL loans. PLUS loans are not eligible for this type of forgiveness.

To qualify for Teacher Loan Forgiveness, you must be employed in an elementary or secondary school in a school district that qualifies for funds under *Title I* of the *Elementary and Secondary Education Act of 1965,* that has been selected by the U.S. Department of Education because more than 30 percent of its students qualify for aid under Title I. Every year these schools are listed in the *Annual Directory of Designated Low-Income Schools for Teacher Cancellation Benefits* published by the Department of Education. (All elementary and secondary schools operated by the Bureau of Indian Education (BIE), or operated on Indian reservations by Indian tribal groups under contract with BIE, qualify as schools serving low-income students even if they are not listed in the directory.) You can check the

Department of Education's online database to see if a school qualified as a low-income school during the years you taught there.

If you begin teaching in one of these schools and it is removed from the *Annual Directory of Designated Low-Income Schools for Teacher Cancellation Benefits* a year or two later, the additional years you teach at that school can be counted toward the required five complete and consecutive academic years of teaching.

The loan(s) for which you are seeking forgiveness must have been made before the end of your five academic years of qualifying teaching service.

Time spent teaching to receive benefits through AmeriCorps cannot be counted toward your required five years of teaching for Teacher Loan Forgiveness.

To receive the full $17,500, you must be a highly qualified math or science teacher at an eligible secondary school, or a highly qualified special education teacher who taught children with disabilities corresponding to your area of expertise. This must be certified by the chief administrative officer of your school. You can receive up to $5,000 in loan forgiveness if you were a highly qualified full-time elementary or secondary school teacher. To be a highly qualified teacher, you must have at least a bachelor's degree and be fully licensed by the state in which you are teaching. New teachers must demonstrate their subject knowledge and teaching skills by passing a rigorous state exam. Experienced teachers must meet these standards and also demonstrate their competence in all the subjects they teach.

Teaching service at an education service agency may qualify if the consecutive five-year period includes qualifying service performed after the 2007–08 academic year.

After completing the five consecutive years of teaching, you can apply for teacher loan forgiveness by printing and completing the *Teacher Loan Forgiveness Application*, available on the U.S Department of Education website. The chief administrative officer of each school at which you taught must complete the certification section. (If you taught at more than one school during the same academic year, the chief administrative officer from one of the schools may complete the certification section. Return the completed application to your loan servicer. If you are applying for forgiveness of loans held by different loan servicers, you must submit a separate form to each of them.

Amounts forgiven through teacher loan forgiveness are not considered taxable income by the IRS.

Perkins Loan Forgiveness

Perkins loan borrowers who perform certain types of public service or are employed in certain occupations can get a percentage of their loans cancelled for each year of service. These public service occupations include:

- Volunteer in the Peace Corps or ACTION program (including VISTA)
- Teacher
- Member of the U.S. armed forces (serving in area of hostilities)
- Nurse or medical technician
- Law enforcement or corrections officer
- Head Start worker
- Child or family services worker
- Professional provider of early intervention services

You also qualify for deferment while performing the service that qualifies for Perkins loan cancellation. Contact the school that you were attending when you received the Perkins loan to find out whether you qualify for any of these programs and how you can apply for deferment and loan cancellation.

Armed Services Loan Repayment Programs (LRP)

Loan Repayment Programs (LRPs) are an enlistment incentive authorized by Congress. Each branch of the Armed Services has different benefits and requirements, and the amount that is repaid depends on the type of service. You must be enlisting for the first time, and you must sign up for an LRP as part of your enlistment contract. To qualify, you must have a high school diploma and a score of 50 or higher on the Armed Services Vocational Aptitude Battery (ASVAB) and enlist for a minimum of three years.

To participate in an LRP, you must also sign a form waiving your education benefits under the Montgomery GI Bill. However, if you reenlist for a second tour of duty, you can reinstate your eligibility for the GI Bill.

To qualify for the Army LRP, you must enlist in one of the critical military occupational specialties (MOS). These MOS change quarterly, so check with your recruiting officer. After one year of active service, the Army will repay 33 1/3 percent of the student's outstanding principle balance or $1,500, whichever is greater (15 percent and $500 for service in Army National Guard and Army Reserve), every year, up to a total of $65,000 ($20,000 for reservists).

The Navy's LRP is available to all active Navy enlisted positions and will also pay for up to $65,000 of loans acquired from a post-secondary education.

The Air Force College Loan Repayment Program (CLRP) pays off a maximum of $10,000 in student loans.

All federal student loans, Perkins loans, and some state loans are eligible for LRPs. Parent PLUS loans that were used to pay for the recruit's education are also eligible for repayment. However, a loan taken out by the recruit for a spouse or relative's education does not qualify.

Discuss your situation with your recruiter during the enlistment process to guarantee that you can qualify for an LRP.

Early Repayment

There is no penalty for early repayment of federal student loans. Study the terms and conditions of a private loan to learn if you will be charged a penalty for paying the loan off early. You will find instructions for early repayment on your student loan servicer's website, or you can call and make arrangements with a customer service representative.

Though paying off student loans early will save you thousands of dollars in interest, it is important to balance your financial priorities. It might make financial sense to continue making the regular fixed student loan payments while allocating extra income to other purposes. Most students also graduate with credit card debt which has much higher interest rates. Paying off high-interest debt takes priority over paying off lower-interest student loans early.

Before you decide whether to pay off your student loans early, calculate the amount you will save in interest and weigh that against the financial benefits of investing for retirement, buying a home, or going back to school to further your education. A worker who contributes to a retirement savings account (such as a 401K or an IRA) while in his or her 20s will earn considerably more for retirement than someone who does not begin contributing until age 30 or 40. If an employer offers matching funds for a 401K, the financial reward is even greater. If housing prices are low, it might be financially sound to purchase a home and build equity in it. A financial planner can help you decide whether to pay off your student loans early, or continue making the monthly payments while you direct part of your income to some kind of investment.

Death or Disability of a Student Loan Borrower

A federal student loan is canceled if the student borrower dies or becomes permanently disabled before the loan is completely repaid. A Parent PLUS loan is canceled if either the student or the parent borrower dies, but not if the student becomes disabled. Depending on the private lender's policy, the responsibility for repaying a private student loan could be passed on to the borrower's heirs.

Contact your student loan servicer for a Death Discharge form to officially notify the Department of Education that the borrower has passed away. You will be asked to send in a certified copy of the death certificate.

Your federal student loan may be discharged if the student borrower is determined to be totally and permanently disabled and meets certain requirements during a three-year conditional discharge period. You must provide a physician's statement that the student became totally and permanently disabled after the loan was made. Details about the requirements for a disability discharge are given on the *Borrower's Rights and Responsibilities Statement* that accompanies your *Master Promissory Note*.

Check to see if the private lender offers a death discharge or permanent disability protection. Sallie Mae's Smart Option Student Loan, New York HESC's NYHELPs loans, and Wells Fargo private student loans all offer death and disability forgiveness policies, but many private lenders do not.

If a private student loan does not have death and disability forgiveness, the lender will first try to collect from the deceased borrower's estate. If there is no estate, the lender will attempt to collect from a co-signer. If there is no co-signer, depending on the community property laws in your particular state, a spouse could become responsible for repaying a student loan. Many community property states have exceptions for education debts so that a spouse who is not a co-signer is not responsible for repaying a student loan.

Student Loan Cancellation

You cannot get your student loan cancelled because you did not like your school, because you dropped out, or because you did not get the job you expected. There are special situations, however, in which a government student loan can be cancelled and your student loan debt discharged. If you believe you qualify for one of these cancellations, contact your student loan servicer to find out what steps to take.

Closed school
Your school closed before you completed your program, or within 90 days after you withdrew, and you were not able to complete the course of study. You are not eligible for this discharge if you are completing your course at another educational institution. You also are not eligible if you completed the course of study but did not receive your diploma. Contact your student loan servicer for a closed school discharge application.
Contact the state licensing agency in the state in which the school was located to ask whether the state made arrangements to keep your

academic and financial aid records. You will need these records to substantiate your claim for a loan discharge, to apply for academic credits when you enter another school, or to prove that you earned a degree or certification.

Forged signature on the promissory note
The school signed your name on the application or promissory note without your authorization, or the school endorsed your loan check or signed your authorization for electronic funds transfer without your knowledge, and the proceeds of the loan were not delivered to you or applied to charges you owed to the school.

False certification
Your school falsely certified that you were eligible to get the loan. A school should not certify a loan to a student who cannot qualify for the occupation for which he or she is being trained because of a mental or physical condition, age, or a criminal record. For example, a person who is legally blind cannot be trained as a truck driver. This cancellation also applies to a school that falsely obtained federal loans for students when the school was not accredited or licensed under state regulations.

Identity theft
Your loan was falsely certified by someone who stole your identity. You will have to prove that your identity was stolen.

Unpaid refund
You withdrew from school but the school did not refund federal loan money that it owed to the Department of Education under its written policy or federal student loan regulations. For example, if your federal student loan was applied to your tuition bill, and you withdrew from classes before the school's withdrawal deadline, all or a portion of that money should be refunded to the Department of Education because you were no longer enrolled in classes. Check the school's federal student aid refund policies.

Bankruptcy

Unlike other types of personal debt, student loans cannot be discharged in bankruptcy. In 2005, Congress extended this status to private student loans.

You can get student loans discharged in bankruptcy only if you can successfully demonstrate to the court that paying your student loan will create undue financial hardship for you and your dependents. To do this, you must bring a separate Complaint to Determine Dischargeability action in the bankruptcy court.

The courts in the Second, Third, Fourth, Fifth, Sixth, Seventh, Ninth, Tenth, and Eleventh Circuits use the Brunner test (Brunner v. New York State Higher Educ. Servs. Corp., 831 F. 2d 395 (2d Cir. 1987)) to decide whether you can discharge your student loans. The Brunner test includes three standards:

- Poverty - Your current income does not allow you to maintain a minimal standard of living for yourself and your family.
- Persistence - Additional circumstances indicate that your current financial difficulties are likely to continue for a significant part of the repayment period.
- Good faith - You have made a sincere effort to repay your student loans.

The Eighth Circuit and most courts in the First Circuit use the "totality of the circumstances" standard, which looks at all relevant factors in your case to determine if it is an undue hardship for you to repay your student loans.

Most courts will discharge the entire loan in bankruptcy if they determine that you qualify. In some cases, the courts will discharge only a portion of the loan; for example, portions of a private loan that were used to pay for living expenses or a purchase not directly related to education.

Student lenders aggressively defend against the discharge of the loans in bankruptcy, so you will probably need to hire a lawyer. You could end up paying almost as much in legal fees as the amount of the loan being discharged.

Courts in different states have different definitions of "undue hardship" and "a minimal standard of living." The court expects the applicant and his or her family to do everything they can to maximize their income and minimize expenses. The court will look at the types of jobs held by the borrower and his or her spouse and may deny the discharge if it believes the applicant could seek a higher-paying job. It might question how much the family spends on specific personal expenses like buying clothes, taking the children on outings to McDonalds, or extracurricular activities such as music lessons. The court will also question whether your current difficult circumstances are likely to continue. For example, if you claim alcoholism as a permanent disability that will prevent you from rising above your present financial situation, the court might deny your application on the grounds that you could better your circumstances by choosing to undergo treatment.

Under Chapter 13 bankruptcy, you might be able to reduce the size of your monthly student loan payment for three to five years, but you will still be responsible for paying off the remaining balance of the loan afterwards.

Bankruptcy is intended to give distressed borrowers a financial fresh start and allow them to actively participate again in the national economy. As the cost of education increases and more students graduate with larger amounts of debt, economists are concerned that a large number of young adults will never emerge from the cycle of poverty and be able to save enough for large purchases such as homes or cars. Changes to the law barring student loans from discharge through bankruptcy are under discussion at many levels.

Drug Convictions

Drug use is rampant on many college campuses in spite of the efforts of school authorities, and an immature young person can easily make unwise choices. Your student could lose access to federal and state financial aid and student loans if he or she is arrested for possessing or selling drugs while attending school. In addition, he or she will probably be evicted from student housing and may be subject to disciplinary action or penalties imposed by school policies. Make sure your student is aware of the risk, and is familiar with the school's drug policy. Remind him or her that associating with drug users and drug dealers could lead to an arrest just by being in the wrong place at the wrong time.

A drug conviction puts you at financial risk, because if your student suddenly loses access to student loan money, you will have to find alternative funding until his or her eligibility is restored. Depending on the date of the conviction, your student may be required to immediately repay part of the loan money he or she has received for that semester. In addition, you might have to come up with a deposit and rent for off-campus housing, and possibly pay for legal fees or a drug rehabilitation program. Your student will face the stress and worry of a court case and financial uncertainty, which will affect his or her academic performance and may lead to withdrawing from school. The drug conviction on your student's record will disqualify him or her for certain types of jobs, particularly in health care, law, and finance. If your student is pursuing a major in one of these fields, the school may have additional requirements for rehabilitating his or her record after a drug conviction.

The following information may be helpful:

If you are convicted of selling or possessing illegal drugs while you are receiving federal student loans, grants, or work study, your eligibility for federal loans and financial aid will be suspended, and you may have to repay some of the grant and loan money you have received. Tobacco and alcohol are not considered illegal drugs

The period of suspension begins on the date of your conviction. The length of the suspension depends on whether you are convicted of selling drugs or possessing drugs, and whether you have previous offenses. For possession of drugs, the suspension is one year for your first offense, two year for a second offense, and indefinite for repeated offenses. For sale of illegal drugs, the suspension is two years from the date of a first conviction, and indefinite for repeated offenses.

You can end the suspension early by participating in an approved drug rehabilitation program. The rehabilitation program must include at least two unannounced drug tests. The program must qualify to receive federal or state funding, or be administered or recognized by a federal, state, or local government agency or court, or by a federally or state-licensed hospital, health clinic, or medical doctor.

A drug conviction does not affect your eligibility for financial aid or student loans if:

- The offense occurred while you were not enrolled in school and receiving financial aid, such as during summer vacation.
- It occurred while you were a juvenile and you were not tried as an adult.
- The conviction was reversed, set aside, or removed from your record.

If you are convicted of a drug offense, contact a financial aid officer at your school to find out whether you must return any financial aid, and how to restore your eligibility through a local drug rehabilitation program. When you complete the drug rehabilitation program, notify your financial aid officer immediately so that your financial aid and loan eligibility can be reinstated.

When you fill out your FAFSA, you are asked whether you had a drug conviction for an offense that occurred while you were receiving federal student aid. If the answer is yes, you will be directed to fill out a *Student Aid Eligibility Worksheet* to determine whether you are eligible to receive federal student aid. Even if you are not eligible for federal student financial aid, you should complete the FAFSA because it is used by schools to determine whether you qualify for school-based financial aid and private loans. Knowingly and intentionally giving false information on a FAFSA is a criminal offense that could lead to fines and imprisonment, and create personal records that could affect your future career. If you are convicted of a drug-related offense after you submit the FAFSA, you might lose eligibility for federal student aid, and you might be liable for returning any financial aid you received during a period of ineligibility.

If you have questions about a drug conviction, you can speak confidentially with a representative of the Federal Student Aid Information Center at 1- 800-4-FED-AID (1-800-433-3243).

Student Loan Repayment Strategies

The best way to pay off a student loan is as quickly as you can. Several calculators on the Federal Student Aid website will help you understand exactly how much money you will save by paying your student loans off quickly. Paying off student loan debt (and other types of debt) should be a financial priority, so that you can save the money you would have to pay in interest over the years.

Here are some tips for paying off your student loans more quickly:

Let other people help you pay.
If a grandparent or relative wants to help pay for your student's education, the best thing they can do is pay off some of the student loans during the student's senior year or after graduation. Giving cash while a student is still in school can increase the student's assets on the FAFSA and the EFC. Once the student has filled out that last FAFSA, assets do not matter anymore.

If friends and family are planning to give your student graduation presents, suggest gifts of cash to help pay off the student loans. Websites like Depositagift.com allow you to set up a personal web page and invite people to give cash. You can include a request and instructions in your graduation announcements.

When you pay off part of a student loan, be sure to apply the payment to the **loan principal only**, rather than making regular monthly loan payments in advance. Reducing the loan principal reduces the amount of interest you will pay over the life of the loan, and lowers the size of the monthly payment when the grace period ends.

Look for additional sources of cash to pay down the loan.
Do you have something you can sell, such as a stamp collection, broken jewelry, or a musical instrument? Is there a temporary or seasonal job you can do to raise extra cash? Paying accrued interest

and reducing the principal before the loan enters repayment will lower the amount of your monthly payments.

Make extra loan payments.

If you receive a bi-weekly paycheck, two months out of each year you will get three paychecks instead of two. Use this money to make extra payments on your student loan. Do the same with employer education benefits or bonus income. When you make extra payments, specify that they are to be applied only to your loan capital and not to your regular scheduled payments. Paying down your loan capital reduces the amount of interest you pay over the life of your loan. You can ask your student loan servicer to apply a payment specifically to the loan that has the highest interest rate.

NOTE: You must instruct your student loan servicer to apply extra payments to your loan principal.

If you do not tell your loan servicer that you want an extra payment applied to a specific loan, the money will be spread across all your loans and applied to interest as well as loan capital. This will ultimately result in your paying more interest over the life of your loan. Some student loan borrowers have reported difficulty communicating to their student loan servicer about how they want a payment applied to their loans. The U.S. Department of Consumer Finance has compiled the following sample instructions that you can submit to your student loan servicer using the "Contact Us" or "Send a Message" link on your student loan servicer's website. You will have to log into your account first.

Sample Instruction Letter:

I am writing to provide you instructions on how to apply payments when I send an amount greater than the minimum amount due. Please apply payments as follows:

1. After applying the minimum amount due for each loan, any additional amount should be applied to the loan that is accruing the highest interest rate.
2. If there are multiple loans with the same interest rate, please apply the additional amount to the loan with the lowest outstanding principal balance.
3. If any additional amount above the minimum amount due ends up paying off an individual loan, please then apply any remaining part of my payment to the loan with the next highest interest rate.

It is possible that I may find an option to refinance my loans to a lower rate with another lender. If this lender or any third party makes payments to my account on my behalf, you should use the instructions outlined above.

Retain these instructions. Please apply these instructions to all future overpayments. Please confirm that these payments will be processed as specified or please provide an explanation as to why you are unable to follow these instructions.

Thank you for your cooperation.

If your student loan servicer does not follow your instructions or you encounter obstacles trying to specify how you want your payments applied to your loans, the Department of Consumer Finance wants to hear about it. Submit your complaint at Consumerfinance.gov (https://help.consumerfinance.gov/app/tellyourstory).

K

eep looking for a good job. Though a student just out of school might have to take the first job available, he or she should not lose

Keep looking for a good job.
Do not lose sight of the purpose of an education. It takes time and effort to find a rewarding job, and many young people become discouraged and want to give up. It is important to look realistically at the size of the monthly loan payments, and to look for a job or career that will allow your student to pay off the loans and still pursue other life goals.

Do whatever you can to help your recent graduate with the job search.
Many schools host job fairs and recruitment interviews, and maintain websites with job postings, but few go beyond that in helping to place their graduates in good jobs. Recent graduates often find that they are on their own once they leave school. Your child might need coaching and reassurance as he or she tries to enter the job market. If the school has a job search website, your student should check it regularly.

Encourage him or her to maintain contact professors and other mentors who can serve as references. Investigate professional associations and conferences where your student can network with others in his or her field. Review your student's resume and offer the benefit of your own experience.

Take advantage of repayment incentives.
Some loans offer repayment incentives such as a lower interest rate when you sign up to have automatic monthly payments withdrawn from your bank account, or upfront interest rebates. Make sure you make your monthly payments on time so that you do not lose these benefits.

Study all the repayment options, incentives, and terms of your loans.
With a clear understanding of the available options, you can choose the best one for your current financial circumstances, and know what to do when your circumstances change

Enlist in the Armed Services.
If you qualify for a military LRP (see above), you can have up to $65,000 of your student loans paid off.

Volunteer with the Peace Corps.
You can defer principal payments on Perkins Loans and federal Direct Loans (including federal Consolidation Loans, Stafford Loans, and Guaranteed Student Loans [GSLs]) for up to three years while you volunteer with the Peace Corps. You are still responsible for paying interest on unsubsidized loans during this period. (The federal government will pay interest on subsidized loans.) You can authorize a monthly interest payment to be deducted from the $7,425 stipend that is given to Peace Corps volunteers at the end of their service, and use this stipend to help with loan payments when deferment ends. You can also apply to your lender for forbearance on the interest payments. Some private lenders also allow deferment during service in the Peace Corps.

Peace Corps volunteers qualify for a 15 percent Perkins loan cancellation for each of their first two years of service and a 20 percent loan cancellation for their third and fourth years of service. Up to 70 percent of a Perkins Loan may be canceled. A volunteer must serve one complete year (365 days) in order to qualify for this cancellation benefit.

You are responsible for contacting your loan servicer and making arrangements for deferment and interest payments. The Peace Corps only provides certification of your dates of service.

The federal government will not pay the interest on subsidized loans that have been consolidated with unsubsidized loans in a Federal Consolidation loan.

Learn more about volunteering with the Peace Corps at www.peacecorps.gov.

> **NOTE: Your time in the Peace Corps might count towards Public Loan Forgiveness.** If you plan to enter a public service job after you leave the Peace Corps, the time you spent serving full-time in the Peace Corps or AmeriCorps could count towards the ten years you need for Public Service Loan Forgiveness. In order for this time to count, however, you must continue making on-time scheduled payments while you are in the Peace Corps instead of taking an economic hardship deferment. The time will also not count if you make a lump sum payment on your loan from the Peace Corps transition allowance no later than six months after you receive the allowance.

Volunteer with AmeriCorps or become an intern with the Student Conservation Association (SCA).
Volunteers with AmeriCorps State and National programs, NCCC (National Civilian Community Corps), and VISTA (Volunteers in Service to America) can have federal student loans deferred while serving nonprofits, schools, public agencies, and community and faith-based groups. Upon successful completion of a term of service, members are eligible to receive a Segal AmeriCorps Education Award, which may be used to repay student loans or to pay for continuing education. AmeriCorps VISTA members may elect to take a post-service cash stipend instead of the education award. AmeriCorps VISTA alumni who choose the stipend may be eligible for up to 15 percent cancellation on certain types of student loans.

The amount of a full-time education award is equivalent to the maximum value of the Pell Grant for the award year in which the term of service is funded. Volunteers may earn up to two awards. Learn more at the AmeriCorps website (*www.nationalservice.gov/programs/americorps*).

A parent or grandparent over 55 who serves in AmeriCorps can apply his or her Segal AmeriCorps Education Award to a child's or grandchild's student loans.

Each year, the SCA (Student Conservation Association) places over 2,000 interns in conservation, environmental and sustainability-based businesses, public land agencies, national parks, and nonprofit organizations throughout the U.S. Upon completing a term of service (from 17 to 52 weeks), the intern receives an AmeriCorps education award of $1,468 to $5,550, depending on the length of the internship. SCA pays for travel, housing, and basic living expenses during the internship. The education awards are based on availability. Learn more at the SCA website (*www.thesca.org*).

AmeriCorps and the SCA give young people valuable work experience and a chance to build a network of friends and contacts in their fields of interest. They provide training in leadership, and in skills and certifications needed for the job at hand. Some internships lead to jobs with non-profits or government agencies.

You are responsible for making arrangements with your loan servicer for deferment of your federal student loans while you are serving with AmeriCorps or SCA, and for applying the education award to your loan payments. You may have to apply for forbearance for private loans during your term of service.

Education awards are treated as taxable income in the year they are awarded.

Get a job with a federal agency.
Some federal agencies offer student loan cancellation as part of their recruitment incentives. Each agency has its own policies regarding education benefits. Ask the human resources officer if there is a student loan benefit associated with the job you are considering.

Do not let a student loan go into default.
Be aware of the due dates for your loan payments. If you are unable to make a loan payment on time, communicate with your loan servicer and make arrangements for a late payment, forbearance, or a different repayment option that reduces the size of your monthly payment. Defaulting on a student loan hurts your credit score, so that you may have difficulty renting an apartment, getting a job, buying a car, or renewing a professional license.

Chapter 8: Default and Delinquency

Making regular student loan payments is challenging for a borrower who does not have a steady, predictable income or who does not make enough money to pay all the monthly bills. Some borrowers do not understand their obligations under the loan contract, or have difficulty managing their personal finances. Almost three-quarters of students who default on their loans have done so after withdrawing from school and failing to complete their studies. Student loan debt cannot be ignored. If you miss more than one or two student loan payments, there will be consequences.

Federal Direct student loans become delinquent the first day after you miss a payment, and remain delinquent until you bring all your payments up to date. Loan servicers report all delinquencies of at least 90 days to the three major credit bureaus. A student loan delinquency lowers your credit score and makes it difficult for you to rent an apartment, apply for a credit card, or get a good interest rate on a car loan or mortgage.

Federal and state governments act as guarantors for student loans. They have a public responsibility to "exercise due diligence" and make sure those loans are repaid. Your loan servicer will make repeated efforts to contact you and get you to make delinquent loan payments. Soon after you miss a payment, you will begin receiving phone calls, email messages, and letters from your student loan servicer. Do not ignore these and hope the problem will just go away. It is better to contact your loan servicer, explain your situation, and apply for forbearance or negotiate a payment arrangement. Often a recent graduate is not living at the home address where correspondence is sent, and family members do not realize the significance of these letters and fail to forward them. When a letter arrives from a student loan servicer, open and read it right away. It is much easier to deal with a delinquent loan than to rehabilitate a defaulted student loan.

If you do not make any student loan payment for 270 days, and do not make arrangements with your loan servicer for deferment or forbearance, the loan goes into default. (If you are paying off FFEL loans at longer than monthly intervals, the period before your loan goes into default is 330 days.)

Student loan default has serious consequences:

No more financial aid
You are not eligible for additional federal student aid if you want to continue your education.

No deferment or forbearance
You are no longer eligible for student loan forbearance, deferment, or income-based repayment plans.

Bad credit
The default is reported to credit bureaus. You may be denied credit cards, car or home loans, or apartment leases. The interest rate on your existing loans and credit cards might go up. Banks might refuse to allow you to open a checking account. You might have to pay higher premiums for car or home insurance. You might be unable to obtain or renew a professional license. Some employers will not hire you for certain jobs because of poor credit. It will take years to reestablish your credit.

No HUD or VA loans
As long as your student loan is in default, you will not be able to get a HUD or VA loan to buy a home.

No tax refunds
The IRS can withhold your federal and state income tax refunds, including the Earned Income Credit (EIC) and apply them to your student loan debt through a tax offset. The federal government is required to notify you in advance that your tax refund will be withheld. You will receive a letter at the address on your most recent tax return, explaining how you can contest the tax offset if you believe there has been a mistake. You can avoid the tax offset by making payment arrangements or paying the loan in full. If you are married filing jointly, your spouse can recover his or her portion of the tax refund by filing an "injured spouse" claim with the IRS.

Wage garnishment

Through Administrative Wage Garnishment, the federal government can have your employer deduct 15 percent of your disposable pay per pay period to repay your student loan debt. Disposable pay is your remaining wages after federal, state, and local income taxes, Social Security and Medicare taxes, and life and health insurance premiums have been deducted. If you are a federal employee, 15 percent of your disposable pay can be garnished through a Federal Salary Offset. You will receive a letter at least 30 days before garnishment begins, giving you an opportunity to enter into a voluntary repayment agreement or request a hearing to explain why you should not have your wages garnished. Your wages might not be garnished if you can show that doing so would cause you extreme financial hardship, or if you have been working at this job for less than a year, after being laid off by a previous employer. An employer cannot fire you because of wage garnishment. The wage garnishment may continue until all of your student loan debt has been paid off.

If your salary is high, the federal government cannot take more than the equivalent of 30 times the current federal minimum wage.

Social Security benefits taken

The government can take some federal benefit payments such as Social Security retirement benefits and Social Security disability benefits (but not Supplemental Security Income) as repayment for defaulted student loans. The government cannot take more than 15 percent of your total benefit, and it must leave you with a minimum of $9,000 per year in benefits.

Increased debt

Late fees, additional interest, legal fees, collection fees, and court costs will be added to your debt. The amount you have to repay will be up to 25 percent more than the original amount of your student loan.

Legal action

If you do not make any arrangements to repay your defaulted loan, a collection agency will sue you for payment of your student loan. Liens may be placed on your assets, preventing you from selling or buying a house.

Getting Out of Default

When your student loan is placed in default by your loan servicer, the entire amount of the loan becomes due and payable immediately. The Department of Education pays the lender and assigns your loan to its Default Resolution Department (www.myeddebt.com). The Default Resolution Department makes repeated efforts to contact you and make payment arrangements. If you do not respond and fail to make satisfactory arrangements, or do make payments under the new arrangement, your loan will be turned over to a collection agency. The Department of Education offers three options for getting out of default:

Repay your defaulted student loan in full.
Contact the Default Resolution Department (www.myeddebt.com) (1-800-621-3115) for instructions on how to repay your student loan. If your loan was disbursed before June 30, 2010, it could be a Federal Family Education Loan (FFEL) guaranteed by a private agency. To repay a defaulted FFEL loan, contact the guaranty agency. All guaranty agencies and the U.S. Department of Education will allow you to set up regular monthly payments that are both reasonable to the agency and affordable to you. Another option is to borrow the money from another source or use a credit card to pay off the loan in full. Do not take out a high-interest loan to pay off a student loan; you can lock in a lower fixed interest rate with loan rehabilitation or loan consolidation.

Rehabilitate your loan.
To rehabilitate a defaulted student loan, you must contact the U.S. Department of Education and agree upon an affordable payment plan. After you have made at least nine full payments of an agreed amount within 20 days of their monthly due dates over a 10 month period, the U.S. Department of Education will reinstate your loan and return it to regular loan servicing.
Involuntary payments secured from you through wage garnishment or litigation do not count as part of your nine payments.

Once your loan is rehabilitated, you will again become eligible to receive additional federal financial aid, and have access to student loan repayment benefits including deferment, forbearance, income-based repayment plans, and Public Service Loan Forgiveness. The default status will be removed from your loan and will no longer be reported to the national credit bureaus. Your wages will no longer be garnished and your income tax refunds will no longer be withheld.

Your new monthly payments may be higher because late fees and collection fees have been added to the loan principle. Late fees are up to 6 percent of each late installment. A late payment is one made more than 15 days after the due date for FFEL loans, or 30 days after the due date for Direct loans. Collection charges are up to 20 percent of each payment on a defaulted loan.

Consolidate your loans.
Direct loan consolidation allows you to pay off the outstanding combined balance(s) for one or more federal student loans by taking out a new single loan with a fixed interest rate. A defaulted federal student loan may be included in a consolidation loan after you have made arrangements through the Default Resolution Department and made several voluntary on-time payments. Typically, you are required to make at least three consecutive, voluntary, on-time payments prior to consolidation.

If you have an FFEL that was assigned to a guaranty agency, collection or late fees of up to 18.5 percent of the outstanding loan may be added to the principal of the consolidation loan.

Collection Agencies

If you do not make arrangements with the Department of Education to repay a defaulted loan, or you fail to adhere to a repayment arrangement, the Department's Default Resolution Group will assign your loan to a collection agency. You will begin to receive telephone calls, emails, and letters from the collection agency. If you do not reach a settlement, the agency will bring legal action to collect the debt.

Collection agency employees are trained to comply with the terms of the Fair Debt Collection Practices Act which governs collection practices by debt collectors. When the Default Resolution Group is notified in writing of complaints concerning its collection agencies, it reviews the evidence and takes action to correct the situation.

Fair Debt Collection Practices Act

The Fair Debt Collection Practices Act guarantees certain rights to consumers:

- Within five days after a debt collection agency first contacts you, it must send you a written validation notice telling you how much money you owe and how to proceed if you do not believe you owe the money.
- A debt collector may not contact you at inconvenient times or places, such as before 8 in the morning or after 9 at night, unless you agree to it. A debt collector may not contact you at your place of employment if they are informed orally or in writing that your employer does not allow you to receive such calls at work.
- If you want the debt collector to stop contacting you, you can send a written letter instructing the debt collection agency that you do not want to be contacted. Keep a copy of the letter, and send it by certified mail, return receipt requested, so you will have a record of the date it was received. Once the collection agency receives your written notice, it cannot contact you again except to tell you there will be no further contact or to notify you that it intends to take a specific action, such as filing a lawsuit. This letter does not make the debt go away. The debt collector can sue you to collect the debt.
- Debt collectors may not harass, oppress, or abuse you or any third parties they contact. They may not threaten violence or harm, use obscene language, or call repeatedly to annoy you.
- Debt collectors cannot repeatedly call neighbors, friends or family members about your debt.
- Debt collectors may not make false claims, such as telling you they are attorneys or government representatives, telling you that you will be arrested, or misrepresenting papers or forms as legal documents.
- Debt collectors cannot collect any interest, fee, or other charge other than the charges specified in your loan contract.

If a debt collection agency contacts you about your student loan debt, talk to the representative at least once to see if you can resolve the matter by making payment arrangements or agreeing on a settlement.

If you receive notice that you are being sued by the Department of Justice over a defaulted federal student loan, respond immediately. Do not ignore the notice and do nothing, or you may lose the opportunity to defend yourself against actions such as wage garnishment or a lien being placed on your property. If you feel you need an attorney to represent you, look for one who is knowledgeable about student loan debt. Instruct your attorney to act quickly and seek a settlement. Do not hire a debt settlement company; their fees are very high and they can do little more for you than you could do for yourself. A debt settlement company may charge you an additional 20 percent of the amount collected, after late fees and collection charges have already been added to your loan principle.

A federal student loan default never goes away. If you do not reach a settlement or rehabilitate a defaulted the loan, the federal government will continue trying to collect the debt through forced repayment until it is paid off.

Defaulted Private Student Loans

Your private student loan contract specifies what constitutes default and what your repayment options are. Many private student loans go into default when a payment has not been made for 120 days. In some cases, your loan goes into default if you miss just one or two payments. You can also go into default on a private student loan if you declare bankruptcy or default on another type of loan.

If your private student loan goes into default, you could receive a notice that your entire loan is due immediately and must be paid in full. The notice may give you other payment options. Study your student loan contract to find out what your rights are.

A debt collection agency seeking to recover a private student loan does not represent the U.S. Department of Education or any other branch of the federal government. It cannot garnish your wages without a court order, seize your federal or state tax refund, take your Social Security or Social Security disability benefits, or prevent you from receiving federal student aid in the future. It is illegal for a private student loan debt collector to pretend to be from the U.S. Department of Education.

Private student loan debt cannot be discharged in bankruptcy, except under the special circumstances discussed above in the section on Bankruptcy.

Unlike federal student loans, a private student lender will generally need to go to court in order to collect forced payments from you. Your rights vary depending on the state you live in. There is a statute of limitations on the collection of private student debt. Learn more out about your options and your rights from the office of your state Attorney General.

If you have a problem with a collection agency or lender concerning a private student loan, submit your complaint to the U.S. Consumer Financial Protection Bureau (https://help.consumerfinance.gov/app/studentloan/ask).

Chapter 9: Student Loans and Your Taxes

Having a family member in college affects your tax return in several ways. You may be eligible for federal and state tax incentives that compensate lower income families for some of the financial burden of paying for higher education. Interest paid on qualifying student loans during the year can be deducted from taxable income. Some scholarship and grant money has to be reported as taxable income. In addition, there is the question of whether or not you should list your student as a dependent on your tax return.

You can expect to spend extra time on your taxes when you have a student in college or student loans in repayment. Tax preparation software walks you through a series of questions and answers to determine whether you qualify for education-related tax benefits, fill out the relevant tax forms, and calculate the amounts of taxable income, deductions, and credits. If your family finances are complicated - for example, if your student has significant income from a job or investments, or if you are paying some expenses with a tax-advantaged education savings account, you might need professional help to prepare your tax return.

While your student is in school, your primary concern is whether you can claim the student as a dependent, whether you qualify for any of the education tax benefits, and how to report taxable income from scholarships and grants. After your student graduates, when student loans are in repayment, whoever is legally responsible for paying back the loan can claim the student loan interest deduction.

Before you sit down to work on your taxes, you will need to collect some or all of the following forms:

Form 1098-T Tuition Statement - An eligible educational institution (such as a college or university) must send *Form 1098-T* to each enrolled student by January 31, 2013. You might receive a copy of this form in the mail. Many schools make each student's form available on the financial aid section of their websites rather than mailing it out. If your student is receiving scholarships and grants that pay only for tuition, the school might not prepare a *Form 1098-T*. The purpose of the form is to show how much the student paid for qualified education expenses during the tax year. The school may report either payments received (box 1), or amounts billed (box 2), for qualified education expenses. The amounts in boxes 1 or 2 of *Form 1098-T* might be different from what you paid, because they might include refunds or charges for a previous year. When figuring an education tax credit, use only the amounts you paid in 2012 for qualified education expenses. *Form 1098-T* gives additional information for the school, such as adjustments made for prior years, the amounts of scholarships and grants, reimbursements, or refunds, and whether the student was enrolled at least half-time or was a graduate student. If your student attended more than one school during the tax year, you will need a *Form 1098-T* from each school. You will need at least one *Form 1098-T* for each student on your tax return.

Form 1098-E Student Loan Interest Statement – If you paid $600 or more of interest on a qualified student loan during the year, you will receive a *Form 1098-E Student Loan Interest Statement*, from your loan servicer. If you paid less than $600, you will need an account statement of your monthly payments, showing how much you paid in principal and interest each month.

Form 1099-INT Interest Income – If you cashed U.S. EE Savings Bonds to pay for education expenses, you will need a *Form 1099-INT* stating how much interest you received. This form will either be given to you by the financial institution where you cash the bonds, or mailed to you at tax time.

Form 1099-MISC Miscellaneous Income – If you used an education award from AmeriCorps or received some form of student loan cancellation, it will be reported as taxable income on a *Form 1099-MISC*.

In addition, if you are claiming the American opportunity credit, you should have receipts or bank statements documenting what you spent for textbooks and equipment.

You will find detailed instructions for filling out your tax return and answers to questions about tax incentives in *IRS Publication 970, Tax Benefits for Education*.

Who Should File a Tax Return

On your tax return, your taxable income for the tax year is always reduced by two amounts: a personal exemption and a standard deduction. In addition, you may be able to claim one or more (if you have more than one student in the family) of the education tax credits. The amounts are determined each year by the IRS. You can look up these amounts in *IRS Publication 501 (2012), Exemptions, Standard Deduction, and Filing Information.* Your tax preparation software will automatically make all these calculations for you. Since you are dealing with two or more tax returns and several individuals of different ages, it is a good idea to prepare several sets of tax returns to determine which combination yields the lowest taxes or the largest refund for your family as a whole.

You can take a personal exemption for each person listed on your tax return: yourself, your spouse, and each dependent. A student who qualifies as your dependent (under 25, single, receiving more than half his or her support from you) cannot take the personal exemption, even if you do not list him or her as a dependent on your tax return. A student 25 or older can still be claimed as your dependent (qualifying relative) if you provide more than half his or her support during the year. The student does not have to live with you. A student who could be claimed as your dependent cannot claim a dependent on his or her tax return.

The personal exemption is gradually phased out for taxpayers with adjusted gross incomes (AGIs) between $250,000 ($300,000 for married couples filing jointly) and $372,500 ($422,500 for married couples filing jointly).

You do not report your student's earned income on your tax return.

The income reported by you and by your student on your tax returns is one of the factors in determining your EFC for the following academic year.

Should Your Student File a Tax Return?

You can claim the standard deduction only for yourself and for your spouse, if you are married filing a joint return. A student who is a dependent on your tax return can claim a standard deduction on his or her own tax return. The standard deduction for a dependent was $1,000 in 2013.

Your student must file a tax return if he or she had unearned income (such as interest and dividends from investments, capital gains, or income from rental property) exceeding this amount.

A student listed as a dependent on your tax return should file a tax return if his or her earned and unearned income exceeds the amount of your standard deduction for that tax year ($6,100 in 2013). Scholarship and grant money that is not spent on qualified expenses counts as earned income for this purpose. For example, a student who received no income but a $12,000 scholarship in 2013 and spent $5,000 on tuition should file a return to report the remaining $7,000. Remember to count only the scholarships and grants received during that tax year, not the amount awarded for the academic year.

A student who has had income tax withheld by an employer should file a tax return to claim a refund, even if his or her total income is less than the standard deduction.

Work-study earnings are subject to income tax but not to Social Security and Medicare taxes, because the student is enrolled full-time and employed less than half-time. If federal income tax has been withheld from work-study paychecks, the student should file a tax return to claim a refund.

A student who earned tips from which his or her employer did not withhold Social Security and Medicare taxes must file a tax return to report that income. A student who had net earnings of more than $400 from self-employment must also file a tax return.

If your dependent student had only unearned income less than $10,000 (in 2013), you can elect to include this income on your tax return. However, it will be taxed at your income tax rate. Reporting this income on your student's tax return will make it taxable at your student's tax rate. If reporting your student's earned income on your tax return pushes you into a higher tax bracket, your student should file his or her own return.

Claiming Your Student as a Dependent

Full-time students who were under age 24 at the end of the tax year can be claimed as dependents on your tax return.

The IRS defines a student as a full-time student at a school that has a regular teaching staff, course of study, and a regularly enrolled student body at the school, or a student taking a full-time, on-farm training course given by such a school or by a state, county, or local government agency. To be considered full-time, a student must be enrolled for the number of hours or courses the school considers to be full time and must be a student for at least five months during the year. The five months do not have to be consecutive.

By claiming your student as a dependent, you are able to claim a personal tax exemption that reduces your taxable income. (In 2013, your taxable income is reduced by $3,900 for yourself, your spouse, and each dependent claimed on your tax return.) If you have paid any qualified education expenses with taxable income, you can also claim one of the education tax benefits. However, if your family AGI is over $300,000 the benefits of claiming your student as a dependent diminish because all of these tax benefits are phased out.

A student who qualifies as your dependent cannot claim a personal exemption on his or her tax return, even if you do not claim the exemption. He or she cannot claim a dependent on a tax return.

The student must meet all the other IRS requirements for dependency. The student must be your child or stepchild (whether by blood or adoption), foster child, sibling or stepsibling, or a descendant of any of them. The student must live with you for more than half the year. While a student is away at college or traveling on vacation, he or she is considered to be living with you.

Student Loans and Your Taxes

A student older than 24 can be claimed as a qualifying relative, as long as you provided more than half of that student's support for the year, and he or she did not earn more than the personal tax exemption for that year.

To claim your student as a dependent, you must have provided more than half of the student's support during the tax year. This determination can be tricky if your student has earned a substantial amount during the tax year, received a large scholarship, or taken out thousands of dollars in federal and state student loans.

Most students can clearly be claimed as dependents the year they start college because they lived at home for eight months of that year, and probably did not earn very much from a job while they were in high school. Each year after that, you will have to scrutinize where the money for school came from, and who paid how much for what.

Qualified education expenses (tuition, fees, and books and equipments required as a condition of enrollment) paid with scholarships or grants, veteran's educational assistance benefits, and employer-provided education assistance are not counted as part of the student's support.

Other expenses for a college student might include tuition and fees, textbooks, computers and electronics, lodging, meals, groceries, transportation, clothing, furnishings, health insurance premiums and co-pays for medical and dental treatment, and personal expenses.

Expenses paid with loans taken out by your student, when he or she is the sole signer of the loan and legally responsible for repaying it, are considered support provided by the student. If a parent is a cosigner or guarantor for a loan, the support comes from the parent. If somebody else, such as a grandparent, was the cosigner, neither of you provided the support. Divorced or separated parents who share the cost of their child's education may not be able to claim the student as a dependent.

Certain expenses paid with distributions from Coverdell ESAs, QTPs, or trust funds could count as support provided by the student, depending on how they are set up and who is considered the owner of the funds.

In addition to college expenses, you must work out the student's share of your household expenses during the months when the student lived in your home (such as during the summer break). You can use *IRS Publication 17, Your Federal Income Tax, Worksheet 3-1.Worksheet for Determining Support* to help determine who provided more than half of the student's support for the year.

If parents buy a car for the student's use at college, the cost of that car is not considered support provided by the parents unless it is registered in the student's name. The cost of insuring and maintaining the car can be considered support provided by the parents. If the student pays for the car, the cost of the car is part of the student's support.

A student who cannot be claimed as a dependent on your tax return can claim the personal exemption on his or her tax return, and an education tax benefit for any tuition that was not covered by scholarships, grants, or other tax-free assistance.

Remember that a student who cannot be claimed as a dependent on your tax return is still considered a dependent student for financial aid purposes.

Qualified Expenses

Amounts that you pay for rent, food, books, transportation, health insurance, sports, supplies, clothing and other support for your child in college generally do not count as higher education expenses when you are filling out a tax return. Only certain types of education-related expenses, called "qualified expenses," are eligible for education tax benefits. The definition of qualified expenses differs slightly for each type of tax benefit. IRS rules are intended to prevent taxpayers from misrepresenting personal expenses as education expenses, but the down side is that families are not compensated for many of the actual costs of attending college.

> **NOTE: Tax benefits apply only to qualified education expenses.**
> Many first-time college families are not aware that the education tax benefits of a Coverdell education savings account (ESA), prepaid college savings account, IRA, or 401K apply only to qualified expenses. Amounts used for other types of expenses are subject to regular income tax rates and, in some, cases, an additional 10 percent penalty.

For most purposes, the IRS defines qualified expenses as:

- Tuition and fees required to enroll at or attend an eligible educational institution
- Course-related expenses, such as fees, books, supplies, and equipment that are required for the courses at the eligible educational institution. These items must be required of all students in your course of instruction.

Books, supplies, and equipment count as qualified expenses only if buying them is a condition for enrollment at the school and you pay the school directly for them. When professors hand out lists of books required for their classes, and you buy those books from the college bookstore, they do not count as qualified expenses because you can still be enrolled in the school whether you buy the books or not.

The American opportunity credit does allow you to count the cost of textbooks and materials required for classes as a qualified expense. For 529 (QTP) distributions, the amount of room and board specified in the school's COA is a qualified expense.

Even if the following fees must be paid to the institution as a condition of enrollment or attendance, qualified education expenses do not include amounts paid for:

- Insurance
- Medical expenses (including student health fees)
- Room and board
- Transportation
- Similar personal, living, or family expenses

Qualified education expenses generally do not include expenses for any noncredit course or any course of instruction that involves sports, games, or hobbies, unless the course is part of the student's degree program or is taken by the student to acquire or improve job skills. (For example, a sports class taken as part of training to become a physiotherapist or physical education teacher.)

Qualified expenses include only tuition and expenses that you pay during the current tax year. You cannot include expenses paid in December of the previous year for this year's classes, but you can include money you pay in advance for an academic period beginning in the first three months of the next year. Qualified expenses paid with student loan money processed by the school are considered to be paid on the date that the student's account is credited.

Education tax incentives are available only for qualified education expenses you paid out of your own pocket. Every year the school provides you with a *Form 1098-T (Tuition Statement)* stating the amount your student paid for qualified expenses. If your scholarships and grants exceeded this amount, you might not be able to take advantage of the education tax incentives.

NOTE: The amounts reported on your *Form 1098-T* might not be accurate.

Schools use different methods for reporting qualified expenses; some report the amount that was billed, some report the amount that was paid, and sometimes the amount may include a refund or a deduction for fees from a previous year. Occasionally amounts of certain scholarships are included twice on the form. If you believe the *Form 1098-T* you received from the school is in error, refer to your own bank statements and payment records when filling out your tax return. Be sure to keep these records in case the IRS questions the discrepancy between the school's *Form 1098-T* and your tax return. If necessary, consult a professional tax preparer or ask the school for clarification.

Taxable and Non-Taxable Income

Student loans are never reported as taxable income, because you have borrowed the money and will be paying it back. You can claim federal and state education tax benefits for qualified education expenses paid with student loan money if all the criteria for eligibility are met.

The portion of any scholarship or grant, including the Pell grant, that is not spent on qualified expenses is considered taxable income. The school should provide a *Form 1098-T* to all students who receive taxable income from scholarships and grants. The taxable amount is calculated by subtracting qualified education expenses (usually Box 1 or Box 2 on *Form 1098-T*) from the total amount of scholarships and grants administered by the school (Box 4 on *Form 1098-T*). In addition, outside scholarship money that was not spent for qualified expenses may be considered taxable income depending on the terms of the scholarship.

Money received for work-study, or as payment for services performed for the school, is considered taxable income. For example, when a student receives a grant that involves doing research or being a teaching assistant, a portion of that money is treated as wages.

Money from a tax-advantaged college savings account such as a Coverdell savings account (ESA) or a QTP, is tax-free only when it used for qualified expenses. The remainder of that money is taxed as income, even when it is used for room and board, textbooks, and other college expenses.

You are allowed to withdraw up to $10,000 without penalty from a tax-advantaged retirement savings account, such as an IRA or a 401k plan, to pay for qualified education expenses. Any amount that you withdraw and do not spend on qualified expenses is taxed at your current tax rate, plus a 10 percent penalty for early withdrawal.

Interest on Series EE U.S. Savings Bonds is not taxed as income if qualified higher education expenses were paid with it.

The American Opportunity Credit, Lifetime Learning Credit, and Tuition and Fees Deduction

The American opportunity credit, lifetime learning credit, and tuition and fees deduction compensate a taxpayer for qualified education expenses with either a refund or a reduction in taxable income.

If your student is receiving scholarship or grant money, you may not be able to claim a tax benefit for higher education. At most schools, qualified expenses are limited to tuition and certain fees that are charged to all students attending the school. A school typically applies grant and scholarship money to tuition and fees first, and then to other expenses such as room and board. You will be able to claim a tax benefit only if the amount of grant and scholarship money is less than the cost of tuition and fees.

If you paid qualified education expenses for yourself or a dependent on your tax return with student loans or with your own money, you might be able to claim one of these tax benefits. Each of them is slightly different; for example, the American opportunity credit is available only for four years of undergraduate study at a qualified institution, while the lifetime learning credit can be used for any number of years for the same student. You can take the tuition and fees credit only if you paid the money yourself, while the other two credits are available even if the student or a third party made the payment. All of them are phased out for families with higher incomes, but each has a different income limit.

If you are eligible to claim the lifetime learning credit and you are also eligible to claim the American opportunity credit for the same student in the same year, you can choose to claim either credit, but not both. If you pay qualified education expenses for more than one family member, you might be able to take the American opportunity credit for one, and the lifetime learning credit for another. You cannot claim a lifetime learning credit or American opportunity credit in the same year that you are claiming a tuition and fees deduction for the same student.

Calculate how each benefit will affect your taxes and choose the best combination for your family for that year. Use tax preparation software to fill out experimental returns for yourself and for each student in your family. For example, if your family income is just above one of the cut-off points, you could lower your MAGI by having your child claim scholarship money as taxable income on his or her tax return. Your child might pay a few more dollars in taxes, but the various education credits and deductions could lower your taxes by hundreds of dollars.

You cannot use the same expense to claim more than one tax benefit, or claim more than your total qualified education expenses. The following restrictions apply:

You cannot claim an education tax credit for qualified expenses that you deducted elsewhere on your tax return, for example, as a business expense.

You cannot claim an education tax credit on the same qualified education expenses that you used to calculate the tax-free portion of money withdrawn from a Coverdell education savings account (ESA), qualified tuition program (QTP), a 401K or an IRA.

If your student withdrew from school, you can claim an education tax credit for qualified education expenses that were not refunded to you by the school. If you were refunded some portion of the money, reduce your qualified education expenses by the amount of the refund. For refunds received from the school after you file your tax return, refigure your education tax credit and submit an amended tax return.

If you have questions about education tax incentives, you will find detailed instructions for filling out your tax return in *IRS Publication 970, Tax Benefits for Education.*

American Opportunity Credit

The American Opportunity Credit allows you to deduct up to $2,500 from your taxable income for each eligible student in your family. Up to 40 percent of this tax credit is refundable, meaning that you will receive up to $1,000 as a tax refund if you do not owe any federal income tax.

You can deduct only qualified education expenses, but for this credit the definition of qualified expenses is expanded to include course materials needed for your student's classes, even if buying those materials is not a requirement for enrollment at the school. Keep the lists of required textbooks or materials for your student's classes, and the receipts for textbook purchases and equipment rentals, in case you get audited.

The cost of a computer purchased for school is not counted as a qualified expense unless your student is required to buy it as a condition of enrollment in the school. For example, an art and design school might require its students to buy or rent a laptop loaded with specific software from the school.

You can claim this credit for only four tax years per student. The student must not have completed his or her first four years of college before the beginning of the year in which the tax credit is claimed.

You claim the credit for education expenses for yourself or for a student who is listed as a dependent on your tax return, even if those expenses were paid by the student or by someone else, such as a grandparent or other relative. Though they paid the bills, they cannot claim the credit because the student is your dependent.

A student who is under 24 at the end of the tax year and is not a dependent on anyone's tax return (such as a married student who files separately) will not receive a tax refund for this credit, but can deduct it from taxable income.

A student who has a federal or state felony conviction for possessing or distributing a controlled substance is not eligible for the American Opportunity Credit.

To receive the credit, you must fill out *IRS Form 8863* and attach it to your tax return. If your answers to the questions in your tax preparation software indicate that you are eligible for this credit, *Form 8863* will automatically be filled out. You will report the amount of qualified expenses listed on the *Form 1098-T* provided by your school, plus whatever you spent on textbooks and materials required for classes.

The American Opportunity Credit is phased out for taxpayers with higher incomes. For 2013, a taxpayer whose modified adjusted gross income (MAGI) is $80,000 or less ($160,000 or less for joint filers) can claim the full credit. The amount of the credit is reduced for taxpayers whose MAGI is between $80,000 and $90,000 ($160,000 and $180,000 for joint filers), and a taxpayer with a MAGI higher than that cannot claim the credit.

The American Opportunity Credit was enacted as part of the American Recovery and Reinvestment Act of 2009 (ARRA). The American Taxpayer Relief Act of 2012 (ATRA) extended it through tax year 2017.

Lifetime Learning Credit

The lifetime learning credit allows you to reduce your taxes by up to $2,000 for qualified education expenses paid for eligible students listed on your tax return. The $2,000 credit is per tax return, not per student. The lifetime learning credit is nonrefundable, meaning that if your eligible education expenses exceed the amount of tax you owe, you will not receive the balance as a tax refund. The credit can reduce your tax to zero, but will not increase your tax refund.

Unlike the American Opportunity Credit, which can only be claimed for four years while the student is an undergraduate, there is no limit on the number of years the lifetime learning credit can be claimed for the same student. The credit can be claimed for graduate and postgraduate programs, as well as for professional courses and classes to acquire or improve job skills. The student does not need to be pursuing a program leading to a degree or other recognized education credential, and does not have to be in school more than half-time. A felony drug conviction does not disqualify the student from receiving this tax credit.

An eligible educational institution is any college, university, vocational school, or other postsecondary educational institution eligible to participate in a student aid program administered by the U.S. Department of Education. This includes most accredited public, nonprofit, and proprietary (privately owned profit-making) postsecondary institutions, and even some schools overseas. The school can tell you if it is an eligible educational institution.

You claim the credit for education expenses for yourself or for a student who is listed as a dependent on your tax return, even if those expenses were paid by the student or by someone else, such as a grandparent or other relative. Though they paid the bills, they cannot claim the credit because the student is your dependent.

For 2013, the maximum amount of the lifetime learning credit is 20 percent of the first $10,000 of qualified education expenses you paid for all eligible students. The maximum amount of lifetime learning credit you can claim for 2012 is $2,000 (20 percent of $10,000). If your MAGI is between $52,000 and $62,000 ($104,000 and $124,000 for joint filers), the amount is gradually phased out. You cannot claim a lifetime learning credit if your MAGI is $62,000 or more ($124,000 or more for joint filers).

Tuition and Fees Deduction

The tuition and fees deduction can reduce the amount of your income subject to tax by up to $4,000. You can take this deduction **only** for tuition and fees that **you paid** for yourself, your spouse, or a dependent for whom you claimed an exemption on your tax return. If someone else paid the tuition and fees, including your dependent child, no one can take the tuition and fees deduction. Even if you do not claim an exemption for your dependent on your tax return, and your dependent paid the tuition and fees, he or she cannot get the deduction.

If tuition and fees were paid directly to the school under the terms of a court-approved divorce decree, they are treated as though they were paid by the student. The student can only claim the tuition and fees deduction for that payment if he or she cannot be claimed a dependent on anyone else's tax return.

In 2013, if your MAGI is not more than $65,000 ($130,000 if you are married filing jointly), you can deduct up to $4,000 in tuition and fees. If your MAGI is between $65,000 ($130,000 if you are married filing jointly) and $80,000 ($160,000 if you are married filing jointly), you can deduct up to $2,000. If your MAGI is over $80,000 ($160,000 if you are married filing jointly), you cannot claim the deduction.

You can deduct tuition and fees paid during the tax year, including anything you paid for an academic period (semester, trimester, quarter, or other period of study) beginning in the first three months of the following year. You cannot deduct tuition that you paid the previous tax year for this year's classes.

The deduction is taken as an adjustment to income on *Form 1040* or *Form 1040A*.

To claim a tuition and fees deduction, complete *Form 8917* and enter the deduction on *Form 1040* or *Form 1040A*.

Student Loan Interest Deduction

 A student loan borrower can deduct up to $2,500 of student loan interest every year from his or her taxable income.

A taxpayer can claim the deduction if his or her MAGI is less than $75,000 ($155,000 if filing a joint return) before student loan interest is subtracted. Only student loan interest paid during the tax year can be deducted. The amount of the deduction is gradually phased out for MAGIs over $60,000 ($125,000 if filing a joint return).

Only the person legally responsible for paying back the loan can claim the student loan interest deduction. If you make payments on your child's student loan, you cannot claim the deduction. Your child, who is legally responsible for paying back the loan, can claim the student loan interest deduction for payments that you made.

You can claim a deduction for interest that you paid on a Parent PLUS loan or other student loan which you took out and are legally responsible for repaying. You must have taken out the loan while the student was your dependent. For the student loan interest deduction, a child or qualifying relative counts as your dependent even if you took out the student loan while you were a dependent on someone else's tax return, or the student was married at the time and filed a joint return with his or her spouse.

Your student cannot claim a student loan interest deduction while he or she is a dependent on someone else's tax return. For example, if you make student loan interest payments for your 22-year-old child while he or she is still in school, neither of you can claim the deduction. Your child is still your dependent until the age of 25, and you are not legally responsible for paying back the loan.

The loan must have been taken out to pay only qualified education expenses for a student who was enrolled at least half-time in a degree program at an eligible educational institution. An institution conducting an internship or residency program that leads to a degree is also eligible.

For the student loan interest deduction, the definition of qualified education expenses includes:

- Tuition and fees
- Room and board (the amount included by the university in its COA, or the amount the student actually paid to live in on-campus housing)
- Books, supplies, and equipment
- Other necessary expenses (such as transportation)

A student loan can be a federal or state student loan, a private student loan, or even a line of credit (such as a credit card) used only to pay qualified education expenses. A loan from a relative or a qualified employer plan does not qualify for the student loan interest deduction.

You cannot claim that you used loan money to pay for qualified expenses that were paid by grants, scholarships, VA benefits, earnings from a Coverdell education savings account, employer-provided assistance, and interest from U.S. savings bonds.

Scholarships, loans, and assistance disbursed through your school will fit within the definition of qualified expenses because they do not exceed the school's COA. If money is disbursed directly to you from other sources, you are responsible for keeping accurate records and receipts.

To qualify as a student loan, the money from the loan must have been used to pay qualified education expenses within a reasonable period of time, defined as within 90 days before the start of an academic period and 90 days after the end of the academic period. Federal and state student loans processed through the school automatically meet this requirement. The definition of a reasonable period of time can be modified if the circumstances are legitimate.

Interest paid through certain student loan repayment assistance programs, such as the National Health Service Corps (NHSC) Loan Repayment Program, and the AmeriCorps education award, does not qualify for the student loan interest deduction.

You cannot claim the student loan interest tax deduction on your tax return in any tax year you are claimed as a dependent by another taxpayer. For this reason, it is better to wait and pay accrued interest on your student's loans in the year your student is no longer a dependent on your tax return, either because he or she has left school or provides more than half his or her support. Then the student will be able to claim the student loan interest deduction on the accrued interest.

Calculating the student loan interest deduction

Your student loan servicer is required to provide you with a *Form 1098-E* by January 31 of each year, showing how much you paid in student loan interest and principal during the previous year. This is not necessarily the amount you will claim for the student loan interest deduction. You are allowed to include the following in your student loan interest:

Loan origination fees

For each student loan, you were charged a loan origination fee that was withheld when the loan was disbursed. you can allocate this loan origination fee over the number of months you will be repaying the loan. For example, if your loan origination fee was $300 and the term of the loan is 10 years, you can add $30 ($2.50 per month) to the student loan interest each year. This applies only to loan origination fees, not to service fees or processing costs.

Perkins Loans do not have any fees.

Federal Direct PLUS Loans for undergraduates carry a 4% fee.

Fees for Direct Subsidized and Unsubsidized Loans will increase to 1.051% (from the previous 1%) and Federal PLUS Loans (for parents or grad students) will be 4.204% (from the previous 4%).

Capitalized interest

If you do not pay the interest that accrues while you are in school and during the six-month grace period, it is capitalized - added to your principal - when your loan goes into repayment. Every month, you make an involuntary interest payment when you pay the monthly interest on the remaining principal. For the student loan interest deduction, you can also make a voluntary interest payment, in which you choose to allocate all of your loan payment to the capitalized interest. The first year, you can add your capitalized interest to the student loan interest deduction. You cannot exceed the total amount of payments that you made on that loan for that year. If there is capitalized interest left over, you can claim it on the next year's student loan deduction.

Loan Forgiveness and Loan Cancellation

After you complete 25 years of payments under an Income-Based Repayment or Income-Contingent repayment plan, the balance of your loan will be cancelled. In the year that your loan is cancelled, the remaining balance is counted as taxable income by the IRS. Cancelled student loan amounts over $600 must be reported on your tax return on *IRS Form 1099C*.

NOTE: IBR means an added tax burden.
For the year that the remainder of your student loan is cancelled under Income-Based Repayment (IBR), you could have an unexpected tax burden because the amount of the cancellation is added to your taxable income. The federal government is now discussing whether to grant tax relief for IBR student loan cancellation. Keep watching for news of this type of relief. If it is not granted, you will have to plan for an extra tax payment that year!

After you complete 120 on-time student loan payments (10 years) under the Public Service Loan Forgiveness program, the balance of your student loan will be discharged. Amounts forgiven under Public Service Loan Forgiveness, the National Health Service Corps Loan Repayment Program, teacher loan forgiveness, and law school loan repayment assistance programs are not considered taxable income by the IRS.

If your student loan is cancelled because of the borrower's death or disability, or because of false certification, a closed school, or any of the situations discussed in the Student Loan Cancellation section, those amounts are taxable income. Each state treats student loan forgiveness differently. Cancelled student loan debt may or may not be subject to state income tax.

Conclusion

The rapid increase in the cost of attending college has made it difficult for many families to pay for higher education without borrowing. At the same time, a college degree is now a requirement for success in many careers. Student loans make it possible for young people to get the education they need, but it is a "buy now, pay later" proposition. Many graduates now enter the workforce with a substantial debt burden that will affect them for the next 10 to 25 years, and may hamper their ability to achieve financial security.

In our modern work environment, the rules for achieving financial security are rapidly changing. The responsibility of saving for retirement is increasingly left to the individual, as guaranteed pension plans give way to IRAs subject to the ups and downs of the stock market. Workers are competing with cheaper overseas labor in well-paid fields like engineering and accounting. The average graduate will change jobs and careers several times during his or her working years. Each change is accompanied by an interruption in income and benefits, but the student loan payments never go away. Though most high school graduates and college freshmen are not worrying about their old age, the decisions they make now could have a significant impact on their future well-being. It is important for their more experienced parents to oversee the process of choosing a school, borrowing to pay for education, and budgeting for school expenses.

While the student is the person legally responsible for the loans he or she borrows, student loan debt affects the whole family. Your student may have to live at home after graduating to make ends meet. As parents, you may decide to step in and help with loan payments or other financial obligations at times when the student is not making enough income. Those dollars would otherwise have gone into your own retirement savings, towards the needs of other family members, or into maintaining the value of your home. Student loan debt could affect your child's ability to help you later in life. Even if your child is not anticipating the consequences of taking on debt, you should be fully informed. You can help your child avoid the pitfalls of taking on too much debt and plan successfully for loan repayment.

Conclusion

Student loans are offered to every student whose family fills out a FAFSA. Though the fine print of the Master Promissory Note spells out the rules, many young people are not fully aware of the risks they face if they do not do well in school, or the consequences if they fail to make loan payments after they graduate.

This book is only a beginning. Once you have evaluated your student's situation, seek out the information you need to plan for the years ahead. Keep asking questions until you are fully satisfied that you understand. A wealth of information is available on the Internet on federal and state government websites, the websites of universities and student advocacy groups, and web sites like Finaid.org. You can also get assistance for a high school guidance counselor, a financial aid officer at your student's prospective university, or a qualified financial professional. The Further Reading section at the end of the book lists web sites where you can find useful information on many student loan topics.

Your student can succeed. You have worked hard to prepare your child for many aspects of life. I hope this book will equip you to offer the same support as your child pursues his or her dreams and transitions to the responsibilities of adulthood.

Further Reading

Academic Progress
Freshman Retention Rate by School. U.S. News and World Report (http://colleges.usnews.rankingsandreviews.com/best-colleges/rankings/national-universities/freshmen-least-most-likely-return)

Mapping Your Future is a national nonprofit organization providing career, college, financial aid, and financial literacy information and services for students, families, and schools. (http://mappingyourfuture.org)

AmeriCorps and SCA
AmeriCorps. Corporation for National and Community Service. (http://www.nationalservice.gov/programs/americorps)

AmeriCorps Loan Deferment Overview (https://my.americorps.gov/trust/help/member_portal/loan_deferment_overview.htm)

The Student Conservation Association (www.thesca.org)

Bankruptcy
Bankruptcy. Student Loan Borrower Assistance (The National Consumer Law Center's Student Loan Borrower Assistance Project) (www.studentloanborrowerassistance.org/bankruptcy)

Debt Collectors
Debt Collection . Federal Trade Commission (www.consumer.ftc.gov/articles/0149-debt-collection)

Default
Federal Student Aid Ombudsman Group, U.S. Department of Education (https://studentaid.ed.gov/repay-loans/disputes/prepare/contact-ombudsman)

File a Student Loan Complaint. Consumer Financial Protection Bureau. (https://help.consumerfinance.gov/app/studentloan/ask)

Rhodes, Steve. *Being Sued for a Federal Student Loan? Don't Panic. Read This!* GetOutofDebt.org. July 26, 2013 (http://getoutofdebt.org/53373/being-sued-for-a-federal-student-loan-dont-panic-must-read-this)

U.S. Department of Education Default Resolution Group (https://www.myeddebt.com/borrower/)

U.S. Consumer Financial Protection Bureau (www.consumerfinance.gov/paying-for-college/repay-student-debt/#Question-1)
Submit a complaint

Drug Convictions
FAFSA Facts. *How do drug-related convictions affect my student loan eligibility?* Office of

National Drug Control Policy, U.S. Department of Education. (http://www.whitehouse.gov/sites/default/files/ondcp/recovery/fafsa.pdf)

Entrance and Exit Counseling
Exit Counseling Guide for Federal Student Loan Borrowers. Federal Student Aid, U.S.

Department of Education (www.direct.ed.gov/pubs/exitcounselguide.pdf)

FAFSA
FAFSA On the Web (https://fafsa.ed.gov)

Common Errors on FAFSA Applications. Finaid.org.(www.finaid.org/fafsa/errors.phtml)
Maximizing Your Aid Eligibility. Finaid.org (www.finaid.org/fafsa/maximize.phtml)

Federal Student Loans
1-800-4-FED-AID (1-800-433-3243) (http://studentaid.ed.gov)

Federal Loan Programs GovLoans.gov
(www.govloans.gov/loans/type/5)

Federal Student Aid website loan calculators
(www.direct.ed.gov/calc.html)

*Title 4. Subtitle B. Chapter VI.Part 682. Subpart B.Section 682.201. 34
CFR 682.201(a)(3) Eligible Borrowers*
(www.law.cornell.edu/cfr/text/34/682.201)

U.S. Department of Education Direct Loan Page for Students
(www.direct.ed.gov/student.html)

To receive a FAFSA or any Federal Student Aid publication, all of
which are free of charge, contact your institution's education
coordinator, order online at www.edpubs.gov, or visit
www.studentaid.gov/pubs to read publications online.

Financial Aid Professionals
Information for Financial Aid Professionals (IFAP)
(www.ifap.ed.gov/ifap)

Training for Financial Aid Professionals. Federal Student Aid Website
(http://www2.ed.gov/offices/OSFAP/training/index.html)

Loan Calculators
Repayment Calculator, Federal Student Aid. U.S. Department of
Education. (http://studentaid.ed.gov/repay-
loans/understand/plans/standard/comparison-calculator

Interest Rate Calculator. Federal Student Aid website
(www.direct.ed.gov/calc.html)

Loan Cancellation
Teacher Cancellation Low Income Directory
(https://www.tcli.ed.gov/CBSWebApp/tcli)

Military Loan Cancellation
My Army Benefits : Loan Repayment Program
(http://myarmybenefits.us.army.mil/Home/Benefit_Library/Federal_B
enefits_Page/College_Loan_Repayment_Program_%28LRP%29.html)

Military.com. The Armed Services Offer Relief for Student Debt
(www.military.com/Resources/ResourcesContent/0,13964,44245--
,00.html)

Parent PLUS Loans
2011-2012 Federal Pell Grant Program End-of-Year Report
(www2.ed.gov/finaid/prof/resources/data/pell-2011-12/pell-eoy-2011-
12.html)

Peace Corps
Peace Corps - Instructions for Student Loans
(www.peacecorps.gov/learn/whyvol/finben/instructions/)

Pell Grant
2013-2014 Federal Pell Grant Payment and Disbursement Schedules
(www.ifap.ed.gov/dpcletters/GEN1306.html)

Study: More Adult Pell Grant Students, Not Enough Graduating.
Sanchez, Claudio. April 10, 2013
(www.npr.org/2013/04/10/176758085/survey-more-pell-grant-
recipients-are-nontraditional-students)

*Pell Grants boost college access for low-income students but money is
only half the story*. Mitchum, Arnold.
(http://hechingerreport.org/content/pell-grants-boost-college-access-
for-low-income-students-but-money-is-only-half-the-story_9915)

Perkins Loans
Federal Perkins Loan Cancellation and Discharge Summary Account.
Federal Student Aid. (http://studentaid.ed.gov/repay-loans/forgiveness-
cancellation/charts#perkins-loan-cancellation)

Federal Perkins Loan Program. U.S. Department of Education.
(https://studentaid.ed.gov/types/loans/perkins)

Private Student Loans

Bader, Noah. *Bankruptcy Law and Student Loans: Not a Working Relationship*. September 11, 2013. JD Supra Business Advisor.(www.jdsupra.com/legalnews/bankruptcy-law-and-student-loans-not-a-08325)

Equal Justice Works\Student Loan Ranger. *Report Suggests Reforms to Help Private Student Loan Borrowers* (www.usnews.com/education/blogs/student-loan-ranger/2013/09/25/report-suggests-reforms-to-help-private-student-loan-borrowers)

Get Out of Default. Consumer Financial Protection Bureau. (www.consumerfinance.gov/paying-for-college/repay-student-debt/#Module-12:-Private-student-loan-default)

Private Student Loans. Finaid.org (www.finaid.org/loans/privatestudentloans.phtml)

Private Student Loans in Bankruptcy. Nolo.com (www.nolo.com/legal-encyclopedia/private-student-loans-bankruptcy.html)

Student Loan Network (www.studentloannetwork.com/)

When it comes to paying for college, career school, or graduate school, federal student loans offer several advantages over private student loans. Federal Student Aid. (http://studentaid.ed.gov/types/loans/federal-vs-private)

Repaying Student Loans

Consumer Financial Protection Bureau (www.consumerfinance.gov/paying-for-college/repay-student-debt)

Current Interest Rates. (http://loanconsolidation.ed.gov/help/rate.html)

DeLisle, Jason. *Understanding the Full Benefits of Stafford Loans*. January 5, 2012. New America Foundation.

(http://edmoney.newamerica.net/blogposts/2012/understanding_the_fu
ll_benefits_of_subsidized_stafford_loans-62092)

DeLisle, Jason. *Stafford Loans Obsolete and Regressive Due to New
Income Based Repayment.* November 15, 2012. New America
Foundation.
(http://edmoney.newamerica.net/blogposts/2012/subsidized_stafford_l
oans_obsolete_and_regressive_due_to_new_income_based_repayment
-7)

Federal Loan Repayment Programs. Govloans.gov
(www.govloans.gov/loans/type/5)

Federal Student Aid website Interest rates and repayment calculators
(www.direct.ed.gov/calc.html)

Mapping Your Future (www.mappingyourfuture.org/OSLC)

National Consumer Law Center's Student Loan Borrower Assistance
(www.studentloanborrowerassistance.org/)

National Student Loan Data System (www.nslds.ed.gov/nslds_SA)

U.S. Department of Education : Repay Your Loans
(http://studentaid.ed.gov/repay-loans)

State Financial Aid and Student Loans

Deadlines for State Financial Aid Applications
(https://fafsa.ed.gov/deadlines.htm)

State Student Loan Guarantee Agencies. Education Resource
Organizations Directory.
(http://wdcrobcolp01.ed.gov/Programs/EROD/org_list.cfm?category_I
D=SGA)

Statistics

College Guide 2013. Washington Monthly.
(www.washingtonmonthly.com/college_guide/toc_2013.php)
National Institute for Education Statistics
(http://nces.ed.gov/ipeds/datacenter/)

Selingo, Jeff. *The Rise and Fall of the Graduation Rate*. The Chronicle of Higher Education. March 2, 2012 (http://chronicle.com/article/The-RiseFall-of-the/131036)

Taxes

IRS Publication 501 (2013), Exemptions, Standard Deduction, and Filing Information (http://www.irs.gov/pub/irs-pdf/p501.pdf)

Tax Tips: *Off to College*. H R Block.com (www.hrblock.com/taxes/tax_tips/tax_planning/offtocollege.html)

Taxability of Student Loan Forgiveness. Finaid.org (http://www.finaid.org/loans/forgivenesstaxability.phtml)

TEACH Grant

Teach Grant Program, U.S. Department of Education (*studentaid.ed.gov/sites/default/files/**teach-grant**.pdf*)

GLOSSARY

accrue – To be added periodically. Interest accrues on your Unsubsidized Direct loans while you are in school.

Adjusted Gross Income (AGI) – Your income minus certain deductions, reported on your most recently filed IRS Form 1040, 1040A, or 1040EZ.

Administrative Wage Garnishment (AWG) – A federal program that collects payment on student loans by having an employer withhold 15 percent of disposable pay.

AmeriCorps –A federal program that engages volunteers in community service projects and offers an education award

Annual Percentage Rate (APR) – The amount of interest charged annually on a loan

Armed Services Vocational Aptitude Battery (ASVAB) – An exam given to candidates enlisting in the Armed Services. A score of 50 or higher qualifies the candidate for the Loan Repayment Program.

attempted credits – Credits for all classes in which a student enrolls, including classes which the student later drops, withdraws from, or fails.

award letter – A statement of the types and amounts of financial aid that a school is willing to provide for an academic year

award year – The academic year, usually consisting of fall and spring semesters, covered by a financial aid award

capitalized interest – Interest that accrues on a student loan while a student is in school and is added to the loan principal when the loan enters repayment

GLOSSARY

collection agency – A company that specializes in collecting payments on defaulted loans

Cost of Attendance (COA) – The official cost of attending a specific school for an academic year, as calculated by the school

credit score – A number calculated using information in your credit report

Data Release Number (DRN) – A four-digit number in the upper right-hand corner of a SAR that is needed to allow a school to make changes to a student's FAFSA

default – Failure to repay a loan according to the terms in the loan agreement

deferment – The deferral of student loan payments while a borrower is in school or serving in the military or a federal community service program

delinquency – Failure to make a loan payment on time. Your lender will report delinquency to at least one of the credit bureaus.

Direct Subsidized Student Loan – A need-based federal student loan program in which the government pays interest on the loan while the student is in school or in deferment

Direct Unsubsidized Student Loan – A federal student loan program available to any student to pay for school. Interest accrues while the student is in school

discretionary income – The difference between your AGI and 150 percent of the poverty guideline for your family size and state of residence

disposable pay – Income remaining after any amounts required by law to be withheld, such as income taxes, have been deducted

earned credits – Credits for classes which a student completes with a passing grade

Expected Family Contribution (EFC) – An amount calculated from the information provided in your FAFSA that determines your eligibility for financial aid

Federal Direct Student Loan Program (FDSLP) – Subsidized and Unsubsidized Direct student loans

Federal Family Education Loan (FFEL) Program – A federal student loan program that ended on July 1, 2010, in which the federal government guaranteed student loans borrowed through private lenders

Federal Loan Cancellation – Several programs through which the federal government forgives student loans after the borrower works for a certain period of time in a field of public need, such as health care or teaching in low income areas

Fiscal Operations Report and Application to Participate (FISAP) – A report filled out annually by all schools that participate in the Federal Perkins Loan program, FWS program, and FSEOG program

forbearance – A period of time during which student loan payments are suspended while the borrower returns to school or participates in public service. Interest accrues on the loan principal during forbearance.

Free Application for Federal Student Aid (FAFSA) – A form that you must complete annually, online or on paper, that determines your eligibility for financial aid

freshman retention rate – The percentage of freshmen who return to a school as sophomores

General Educational Development (GED) certificate – A certificate equivalent to a high school diploma, issued after successful completion of the GED test

grace period – A six-month period, beginning the day the student leaves school (separation date), during which the student is not required to begin making payments on a student loan.

Grade Point Average (GPA) – An average of a student's grades during a specified time period

grace period – A six-month period, beginning the day the student leaves school (separation date) during which the student is not required to begin making student loan payments

graduation rate – The percentage of freshmen who graduate with a college degree within four or six years

grant – A monetary gift that does not require repayment

Income Based Repayment (IBR) – A student loan repayment program in which the monthly payments are capped at 15 percent of discretionary income, and are adjusted each year

Institutional Student Information Record (ISIR) – An electronic record sent by the Department of Education to a school, with information from the student's FAFSA, including personal identification, information used to calculate the EFC, and the student's EFC

loan period – A period of academic enrollment, such as a semester, during which a student receives a student loan.

Loan Repayment Programs (LRPs) – An Armed Services enlistment incentive authorized by Congress

loan servicer – A company that handles billing and repayment options for student loans

Master Promissory Note (MPN) – A legal document, containing the terms of the loan agreement, that can be applied to multiple student loans from the same lender.

maximum eligibility period – The maximum amount of time that a student can receive Direct Subsidized Student Loans, equal to 150 percent of the published length of the program of study.

modified adjusted gross income (MAGI) – Your AGI with certain tax deductions and exclusions added. Your MAGI determines eligibility for certain tax benefits such as the Hope Scholarship Tax Credit.

National Student Loan Database (NSLD) – The U.S. Department of Education's central database containing information regarding all federal student loans and financial aid

partial financial hardship – The monthly payment on your IBR-eligible federal student loans under a 10-year Standard Repayment Plan is higher than the monthly payment under IBR.

Peace Corps – A federal pro0gram that trains volunteers and sends them to work overseas in areas of need

Pell Grant – A need-based financial education grant for low-income families

Perkins Loan Program – A need-based federal student loan program administered through the schools

PLUS loan – A federal unsubsidized student loan available to graduate students and parents of dependent undergraduate students

principal – The total amount of money borrowed, plus any capitalized interest

private student loan – A student loan offered by a bank or other financial institution that does not offer the low interest rate and repayment benefits of a federal or state student loan

rate of completion – The number of earned credits divided by the number of attempted credits

regular student – A student enrolled for the purpose of obtaining a degree or a certificate in an eligible program

Satisfactory Academic Progression (SAP) – A set of standards that determine whether a student is on track to complete his or her degree within a reasonable time period

scholarship – A gift of money to pay for education

Stafford Loan – Federal Direct student loan

Student Aid Report (SAR) – A summary of the information in your FAFSA and your eligibility for student aid

Student Conservation Association (SCA) – A non-profit organization offering conservation internships that are eligible for AmeriCorps education awards

tax offset – An amount withheld by the IRS from a tax refund to repay a defaulted student loan

Teacher Education Assistance for College and Higher Education Grant Program (TEACH) – A federal program that gives grants of up to $4,000 a year to students who are completing or plan to complete course work needed to begin a career in teaching

TRIO – Eight federal programs designed to motivate, support, and provide services for students from disadvantaged backgrounds

VISTA – A federal program to engage volunteers in fighting poverty that comes under AmeriCorps and offers and education award